Contented Calf

Nourishing recipes for breastfeeding mums

To help promote milk production

Elena Cimelli and Jassy Davis

This book is published by
Grosvenor House Publishing Ltd
28-30 High Street, Guildford, Surrey GU1 3HY
www.grosvenorhousepublishing.co.uk

A CIP record for this book is available from the British Library

ISBN 978-1-908105-52-3

*The Contented Calf Cookbook: Nourishing recipes for breastfeeding
mums* reflects the author's experience and is provided for general
reference and educational purposes. It is not intended to be a substitute
for medical advice or counselling. It is important to inform your doctor,
health visitor, dietician, lactation consultant or any other medical advisor
you feel appropriate of your issues and concerns with regards
to breastfeeding and low milk production so you and your baby's
health can be followed closely by a qualified health care professional.

Increased milk supply following the consumption of the dishes in this
book is not guaranteed and any results experienced will be different
from person to person. Breastfeeding is a complex process, with diet
only being a small part of the picture. A list of references, detailing the
principles of lactogenic food, breast milk production and supply, used
to help put together *Contented Calf Cookbook: Nourishing recipes
for breastfeeding mums* can be found at the back of the book, along
with suggested further reading.

Neither the publisher nor the author takes any responsibility if the
contents of this book are taken as a recommendation. Neither of
the authors are medically educated, trained or qualified. You and your
doctor take full responsibility for the use that you make of this book.

Author Elena Cimelli

Recipes Jassy Davis

Photographer Tony Briscoe

Food stylist Penny Stephens

Book design and art direction
www.stevensoncreative.co.uk

Contents

Foreword from Hilary Jacobson

I first began talking about lactogenic foods and herbs in an online forum for mothers with low milk supply in 2000.

At that time, the idea that what we eat and drink could help mothers build and maintain their milk supply seemed revolutionary. And yet, it's not new at all. This knowledge is as old as humanity and is found in the collective experience of women around the world.

After reading my book, *Mother Food*, which explores these world traditions, Elena experimented with lactogenic foods while breastfeeding her own baby. She enjoyed creating meals and seeing the benefits for her milk supply and health. Inspired to share such delicious recipes with other breastfeeding mothers, Elena worked with her friend Jassy to develop this lactogenic foods cookbook.

Lactogenic foods enjoy a long tradition in Britain. The botanist, herbalist and physician Nicholas Culpeper mentions a dozen lactogenic herbs and foods in his books *The English Physician* and *The Complete Herbal*, published over 350 years ago.

In 1850, the London Obstetrician/Gynaecologist Dr Charles Henry Felix Routh published the first popular book on breastfeeding, *Infant Feeding and Its Influence on Life*. Routh's work was so all encompassing and accurate that 80 years later, breastfeeding books still copied large portions of its content.

Remarkably, Routh wrote a lengthy chapter on the causes of low milk supply and the foods and herbs that he personally had observed help mothers increase their supply. These foods and herbs are all here in this collection of wholesome meals and tasty desserts for the breastfeeding mother.

Today, as mothers garner the benefits of a lactogenic diet for their milk supply and health, we naturally feel inspired to become creative and to make these foods and herbs our own. Elena Cimelli's cookbook is a wonderful example of how breastfeeding mothers can embrace these special, healthful foods. Enjoy the adventure of seeing how these tasty, wholesome additions to your diet can enhance your experience as a breastfeeding mother.

Hilary Jacobson

Author, *Mother Food: A Breastfeeding Diet Guide with Lactogenic Foods and Herbs for a Mom and Baby's Best Health*

Welcome

When it came to breastfeeding, I was incredibly lucky. Fifteen minutes after my daughter made her entrance into the world, she was latched on to my breast and there she stayed for much of the next 10 months.

But one of my friends didn't have such a good tale to tell. Her son spent his first week in a Special Care Baby Unit and this severely affected her milk supply. She faced an uphill struggle moving him from being bottle fed to being fully breastfed. Armed with a breast pump and the internet, she did whatever she could to build up her milk supply.

During one of her internet trawls she found out about foods and herbs that can help with milk supply. She told me about it and I was intrigued. I started searching for recipes that used these lactogenic foods, but there were only a few out there.

This got me thinking. In the run up to our daughter's birth my husband and I had cooked up a storm and filled our freezer with meals that we could just bung in the oven once we were in the throes of new parenthood. I wondered if I could've made those meals with lactogenic ingredients.

And that's how this book began life. I know from experience that most new parents don't have the time or energy to slave away in the kitchen. Getting ahead, stocking up your fridge and freezer, can really take the pressure off once your baby arrives. If you can eat foods that may help improve your chances of successfully breastfeeding, then even better.

The recipes in this book have been developed using lactogenic ingredients. Wherever possible, they're designed so you can make them in the weeks leading up to the birth, freeze them and simply reheat when you need them. You can easily build up a stock of tasty meals, ready for when your baby arrives.

We've also included some quick recipes you can prepare fresh, keeping these as simple as possible. All the recipes are nourishing and full of flavour and they'll appeal to partners, children, friends and non-breastfeeding mums, too.

So turn the page, get started and get stuck in!

Elena Cimelli

what is a lactogenic diet?

Being a new parent is a whirlwind of experiences.
You have a thousand and one questions about how best to
care for your baby and high up on that ever-growing list is feeding.

Breastfeeding is a personal and emotive topic, with every woman having a unique experience of and feelings towards it. I feel incredibly lucky that I was able to successfully breastfeed my daughter exclusively for six months and continue on for another four months once we started to introduce solids. It wasn't all plain sailing, but I'm very grateful I was able to experience the comfort and connection that can come from breastfeeding.

I can't explain why I had a good experience while it can be difficult for others. Breastfeeding is a complex process, with diet only a small part of the picture. But when I look back at what I was eating while I was breastfeeding, a lot of the food happened to be lactogenic – foods that promote breast milk production. I think these foods helped me and perhaps they can help you, too.

Breast milk basics

This book is first and foremost a recipe book. But it helps to know, in general terms, how breast milk production works.

If you look at the diagram on the right, the inside of the breast looks a bit like a bush with the nipple as the base or stump. There are around nine milk lobes per breast, each with a main duct leading from the nipple and multiple smaller ducts forming the lobe itself. The alveoli are round, saclike glands that are lined with milk-producing cells called lactocytes. It's inside each alveolus that the milk is produced, travelling down the ducts and then out of the nipple.

The process of making milk (lactogenesis) involves two hormones – prolactin and oxytocin – and can be broken down into four simple stages:

1 The prolactin receptors on the walls of the lactocyte cells allow the prolactin in the bloodstream to move into the lactocytes and stimulate milk production.

2 As the alveoli fill up with milk they stretch, changing the shape of the lactocytes so they cannot absorb any more prolactin. As well as this, the milk contains a protein called Feedback Inhibitor of Lactation (FIL). When the breast is full, the increased amount of FIL gives the message to the lactocytes to stop producing milk.

3 The baby's suckling stimulates the release of oxytocin, which causes the muscles around the alveoli to contract, squeezing the milk into the ducts, which swell behind the nipple, full of milk.

4 As the milk empties out of the alveoli, the lactocytes return to their normal shape, so prolactin can flow back in and milk production starts again. The milk that is produced further into the baby's feed is higher in fat and more satisfying.

For more information on breast milk production, go to www.contentedcalf.com/breastmilk

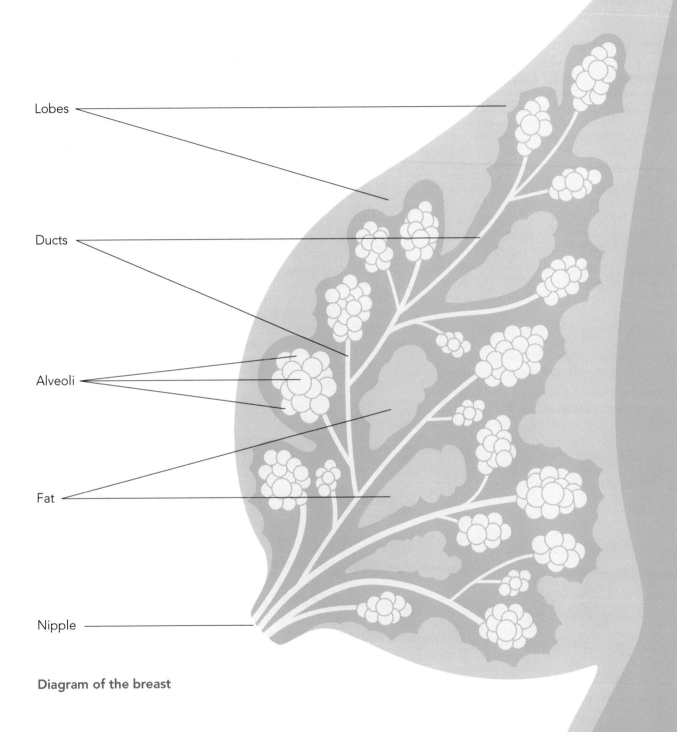

Lobes

Ducts

Alveoli

Fat

Nipple

Diagram of the breast

How lactogenic foods can help

Foods can be considered lactogenic for several reasons. The first grouping features foods that can help promote prolactin. Anything that helps our bodies increase the level of prolactin in our bloodstream can help increase milk supply. Meat, eggs, dairy, many vegetables, nuts, seeds, legumes and grains contain the amino acid tryptophan in high amounts, which promotes prolactin production.

There's also a small group of herbs and foods containing substances that can act as sedatives, which also encourage increased production of prolactin. Foods containing polysaccharides raise prolactin levels in the blood, too.

The other breastfeeding hormone, oxytocin, contracts the muscles around the alveoli, squeezing the milk into the ducts. If production of oxytocin is suppressed, this 'milk-ejection reflex' is inhibited. Stress hormones, such as adrenaline, suppress the production of oxytocin. Ensuring that you eat meals and snacks throughout the day can help reduce your stress levels, as hunger can induce stress.

There are also foods that are thought to help remedy problems with let-down or flow. Hilary Jacobson lists anise, basil, dill, fennel (garden and wild) and lettuce in her book *Mother Food* – a range originally recommended by the 1st century AD Greek doctor Dioscorides.

Breast milk quality

Breast milk draws its make-up from the food you eat, so it's essential to eat foods that make it the best it can be. Two food types worth highlighting are:

Essential fatty acids DHA and other Omega 3 fatty acids are fundamental to the development of the brain in infancy and childhood. Breast milk boosts brain growth because, provided the mother herself eats foods rich in Omega 3 fatty acids, it contains lots of DHA. Having a diet with good levels of DHA in it has also been linked to promoting a mother's own psychological and emotional well-being.

Coconut oil Your body's anti-microbial fatty acid (monolaurin) is made from lauric acid. Monolaurin is anti-viral and anti-bacterial. If you add foods rich in lauric acid to your diet, the amount in your breast milk increases substantially. In countries where coconut oil is part of the staple diet, lauric acid levels in breast milk can be as high as 21% (normally lauric acid makes up 3% of the saturated fats in breastmilk).

The lactogenic list

Foods specifically considered to be lactogenic:

Fats & oils Butter, coconut oil, sesame seed oil, extra virgin olive oil

Fruit Apricots, cherries, dates, figs, nectarines, papayas, peaches, plums

Grains Barley, buckwheat, cornmeal, millet, oats, quinoa, rice (brown and white)

Herbs & spices Aniseed, basil, black pepper, caraway seed, cinnamon, coriander, cumin, curry, dill, fennel, garlic, ginger, marjoram, sea salt, thyme, turmeric

Leafy greens Dandelion leaves, kale, lettuce, rocket, spinach, watercress

Legumes Chickpeas, all beans, lentils and peas

Meat & fish Venison, poultry (especially turkey), most fish and seafood, in particular crab and squid

Natural sugars Honey, malt syrup, maple syrup

Nuts Almonds, cashews, pecans

Seeds Evening primrose, flaxseed, fenugreek, pumpkin, sesame, sunflower

Vegetables Asparagus, artichokes, beetroot, broccoli, carrots, cauliflowers, fennel, Jerusalem artichokes, lettuce, mushrooms, onions, potatoes, spinach, sweet potatoes, Swiss chard.

The anti-lactogenic list

As well as foods and herbs that can help improve milk supply, there are those that may decrease supply, particularly if consumed in large quantities or eaten exclusively. Most mothers will not be affected by eating these foods, but as some are, it's worth noting them.

Caffeine An increase in stress hormones can lead to the constriction of the capillaries in the breasts and possibly affect supply. Foods and drinks containing caffeine, which increases stress hormones, can be problematic, such as black tea, coffee, green tea, caffeinated soft drinks and chocolate.

Astringent foods These can cause sensitive tissue to constrict and can also lead to restricted blood circulation in the breasts. So citrus juice, citric acid and all foods containing citric acid may need to be avoided or reduced. Included in this group are Vitamin C supplements, sour berries and fruit and red raspberry leaf tea.

Vitamins & additives Anything that increases dopamine, which suppresses prolactin production, is best avoided or eaten in small amounts, in particular Aspartame and Vitamin B6.

Herbs Avoid lemon balm, parsley, peppermint, rosemary, sage, spearmint and thyme in large quantities as they are suspected of drying up a mother's milk supply.

It's also worth avoiding foods that either make your breast milk more difficult to digest or that your baby seems not to like the taste of, such as cabbage, Brussels sprouts and cauliflower, as this may lead to them drinking less and your breasts therefore producing less.

For more information on a lactogenic diet, go to www.contentedcalf.com/breastmilk or read *Mother Food* **by Hilary Jacobson.**

Guide to freezing foods

Stocking up your freezer with home-made meals, snacks and treats means you don't have to worry about feeding yourself when you're concentrating on feeding your new baby – it's all there and ready to go.

Your freezer can be your best friend during those first hectic weeks after your baby comes home. Some days I barely seemed to have time to get dressed, let alone worry about what was for dinner! But in the run-up to giving birth my husband and I filled our freezer with meals we could just bung in the oven, which meant we actually got to eat something delicious and filling every day.

There are 35 freezeable recipes in *The Contented Calf Cookbook* and we've given basic freezing instructions at the bottom of each one, but this guide will help you get the most out of your freezer.

Get the right temperature

Your freezer is probably running at -18°C, which is perfect for storing food. But the faster you freeze food, the better the result. If you can, set your freezer to its lowest temperature 8–12 hours before you put a fresh batch of meals in to freeze. And never put warm food into the freezer – it'll bring up the temperature and other foods could begin to defrost and deteriorate.

Wrap up well

If food isn't properly wrapped it can dry out and develop freezer burn. It'll still be safe to eat but it won't look good and some foods can develop an unpleasant flavour. When you're freezing meals, portion them into freezerproof tubs or foil containers with lids. Liquids can be poured into sealable freezer bags and if you're open freezing something, like the Fig and walnut cookies (page 85), leave them open on a baking tray for 2–3 hours until solid, then pack into freezer bags.

Label, label, label

Many's the evening I've defrosted a meal, not knowing if I'm going to get fish pie or macaroni cheese. Labelling everything with its name, portion size and the date it was frozen can save a lot of head scratching later on. I also write the oven temperature and timings on meals that can be baked from frozen so I know straight away how to cook them.

First in, first out

Freezing food helps preserve it but over time it will begin to lose its flavour. The best plan is to rotate foods in your freezer, defrosting and cooking the oldest food first. We recommend you freeze most of the recipes in *The Contented Calf Cookbook* for no more than three months to get the best out of them.

Thawing & refreezing

Some of the meals in this book can be cooked from frozen and some are better defrosted and then reheated or cooked. The best way to defrost frozen food is overnight, in the fridge if it's meat, poultry or fish. Once food has been defrosted, store in the fridge if you're not cooking it straight away. Bakery and vegetable dishes can be defrosted at room temperature. Once defrosted, keep vegetarian meals in the fridge. Breads and cakes stay fresher at room temperature.

When it comes to refreezing, it's best to be safe and avoid it if possible. Foods can be defrosted, cooked in things like stews or soups and then refrozen, but if you've defrosted a meal it's better to cook and eat it than try to refreeze it.

Recipe guide

All the recipes in *The Contented Calf Cookbook*
are designed to be easy to follow, but here are
a few tips to help you use them.

Ingredients
All the ingredients are listed in the order
in which they're used.

Serving sizes
I've given serving sizes for all the recipes,
usually serves 1, 2, 4 or 6. If a recipe says it serves
4–6 people, that's because I know portion sizes
depend on how hungry you are (I was ravenous
when I was breastfeeding!) and if you're serving
children, they'll need smaller servings.

Doubling up
Most of the recipes can be doubled or even tripled
and will still work well, if you'd like to make a larger
stock of a particular meal.

Symbols Key
There are 59 vegetarian, 31 vegan and
44 gluten-free recipes in *The Contented Calf
Cookbook*. All the recipes have symbols at the
top of them so you can quickly spot which ones
are suitable for you – and also for freezing.
There's a symbols key below to help you
spot them.

SYMBOLS KEY	
V	Vegetarian
	Vegan
	Gluten free
	Freezeable

Get Ahead
If a recipe is suitable for making in advance,
there is a Get Ahead tip on the page telling
you the best way to store or freeze it and
the best way to reheat it, if necessary.
Look out for the clock symbol on the right.

Timings
There are three types of timings at the top of each
recipe: preparation, active cooking and total cooking.

Preparation: This is how long it will take you to
prepare the ingredients. That's chopping, peeling,
slicing, whisking, beating and all similar steps before
you actually start cooking. If an ingredient needs
extra preparation, like overnight soaking or chilling,
it'll also be noted here.

Active cooking: This is the amount of time you'll
spend actually cooking when you can't leave the
dish to simmer or bake away under its own steam.

Total cooking: This is how long, on average, it will
take for the meal to cook, from the first ingredient
hitting the frying pan to the finished meal coming out
of the oven. You may have to stir the pan occasionally
while it finishes cooking – and don't leave pans on
the hob completely unattended – but you won't
have to keep your eyes on the food for the whole
of the total cooking time.

Remember, all timings are approximate.
Food, hobs, ovens and tastes will vary.

Measurement guide

All the recipes for *The Contented Calf Cookbook* were created using metric measurements: grams, kilograms, litres and millilitres. Recipes usually work best in their original measurements, but they're easy to convert if you'd prefer to work in imperial or cups.

Metric to imperial

As a rough guide, 25g is equal to 1oz and 550ml is equal to 1 pint. This isn't an exact conversion (it's really 28.35g and 568ml), but for most recipes these approximate conversions should work. The tables on the right give a longer list of metric to imperial conversions.

Metric to US cups

US cups are easy to use, but there's no quick way to convert grams into cups because different foods come out at different weights. Some of the more common foods are listed in the table opposite, or go to www.recipes4us.co.uk/us_cups_to_weight.htm for a detailed list.

Metric to US liquid measurements

An American pint has 16fl oz compared to 20fl oz in the British pint. Use the US liquid conversions table opposite to swap millilitres to fluid ounces.

Spoon measurements

The recipes were all developed using British measuring spoons. These are usually equivalent to a heaped tablespoon or heaped teaspoon if you prefer to use one from your cutlery drawer.

Measurement tables

Weights

Metric	Imperial
10g	½oz
20g	¾oz
25g	1oz
40g	1½oz
50g	2oz
60g	2½oz
75g	3oz
110g	4oz
125g	4½oz
150g	5oz
175g	6oz
200g	7oz
225g	8oz
250g	9oz
275g	10oz
350g	12oz
450g	1lb
700g	1lb 8oz
900g	2lb
1.35kg	3lb

Dimensions

Metric	Imperial
3mm	⅛ inch
5mm	¼ inch
1cm	½ inch
2cm	¾ inch
2½cm	1inch
3cm	1¼ inch
4cm	1½ inch
4½cm	1¾ inch
5cm	2 inch
6cm	2½ inch
7½cm	3 inch
9cm	3½ inch
10cm	4 inch
13cm	5 inch
13½cm	5¼ inch
15cm	6 inch
16cm	6½ inch
18cm	7 inch
19cm	7½ inch
20cm	8 inch
23cm	9 inch
24cm	9½ inch
25½cm	10 inch
28cm	11 inch
30cm	12 inch

Volume

Metric	Imperial
55ml	2fl oz
75ml	3fl oz
150ml	5fl oz (¼ pint)
275ml	10fl oz (½ pint)
570ml	1 pint
725ml	1¼ pints
1 litre	1¾ pints
1⅕ litre	2 pints
1½ litre	2½ pints
2¼ litres	4 pints

Oven temperature

Gas Mark	°C	°F
1	140°C	275°F
2	150°C	300°F
3	170°C	325°F
4	180°C	350°F
5	190°C	375°F
6	200°C	400°F
7	220°C	425°F
8	230°C	450°F
9	240°C	475°F

US cup conversions

Metric	Imperial	American
110g	4oz	1 cup flour
225g	8oz	1 cup caster sugar
200g	7oz	1 cup brown sugar
225g	8oz	1 cup butter
150g	5oz	1 cup sultanas/raisins
90g	2⅔oz	1 cup porridge oats
150g	5oz	1 cup ground almonds
150g	5oz	1 cup whole almonds
225g	8oz	1 cup uncooked rice
150g	5oz	1 cup dried apricots
110g	4oz	1 stick butter

US liquid conversions

Metric	Imperial	American
15ml	½fl oz	1 tbsp
30ml	1fl oz	⅛ cup
60ml	2fl oz	¼ cup
120ml	4fl oz	½ cup
240ml	8fl oz	1 cup
480ml	16fl oz	1 pint

Breakfasts

A really good breakfast always helps kickstart my day, whether it's thick, creamy porridge or a slice of toast slathered in pecan butter.

6
ways with porridge

Hot, hearty and wholesome, a bowl of porridge is a soothing meal to wake up to.

Soaking the oats overnight cuts the cooking time in half.

V
1 Plain and simple

2 minutes to prepare + soaking | 5 minutes active cooking | Makes 1 serving

Place **40g porridge oats** in a bowl and cover with **100ml cold water**. Cover and soak overnight. In the morning, tip the oats and any water into a small pan and add **100ml whole milk.** Place over a low heat and simmer, stirring frequently, for 5 minutes or until the porridge has thickened. Serve topped with **1 tbsp natural yogurt** and a drizzle of **clear honey**.

V
4 Toasted oat

1 minute to prepare | 10–15 minutes active cooking | Makes 1 serving

Place **40g porridge oats** in a small pan over a medium heat and toast, stirring frequently, for 3–4 minutes or until lightly browned and they smell oaty. Add **200ml whole milk** and a **small pinch of salt**. Continue to cook over a low heat, stirring frequently, for 5–10 minutes or until the porridge has thickened. Serve topped with a spoonful of **natural yogurt** and a drizzle of **clear honey**.

V 🥕

2 Fresh fig and almond

3 minutes to prepare + soaking | 5 minutes active cooking | Makes 1 serving

Place **40g porridge oats** in a bowl and cover with **100ml cold water**. Cover and soak overnight. In the morning, tip the oats and any water into a small pan and add **100ml almond milk** (see page 92 for recipe) and **a pinch of ground cinnamon**. Place over a low heat and simmer, stirring frequently, for 5 minutes or until the porridge has thickened. Serve topped with **1 fresh fig**, sliced, and a drizzle of **maple syrup**.

V 🥕

3 Date, coconut and cardamom

5 minutes to prepare + soaking | 5 minutes active cooking | Makes 1 serving

Bash **3 cardamom pods** with a pestle to break them open. Discard the green skins and grind the seeds to a fine powder. Place in a bowl with **40g porridge oats** and **100ml cold water**. Cover and soak overnight. In the morning, tip the oats and any water into a pan. Add **1 tbsp coconut cream (approximately 25g)**, **6 dried, pitted dates**, chopped, and **100ml more cold water**. Place over a low heat and cook, stirring, for 5 minutes or until thickened. Serve immediately.

V 🥕

5 Spiced almond and dried fruit

5 minutes to prepare + soaking | 5 minutes active cooking | Makes 1 serving

Place **40g porridge oats** in a bowl with **2 soft, dried, ready-to-eat apricots, 2 dried, pitted dates** and **1 soft, dried, ready-to-eat fig**, all chopped, and **100ml cold water**. Cover and soak overnight. In the morning, tip the oats, fruit and any water into a small pan and add **100ml almond milk** (see page 92 for recipe) and a **pinch of ground cinnamon**. Place over a low heat and simmer, stirring frequently, for 5 minutes or until the porridge has thickened. Serve sprinkled with **extra ground cinnamon**.

V 🥕

6 Mango and coconut

5 minutes to prepare + soaking | 5 minutes active cooking | Makes 1 serving

Place **40g porridge oats** in a bowl and cover with **100ml cold water**. Cover and soak overnight. In the morning, tip the oats and any water into a small pan and add **½ medium mango**, peeled, stoned and chopped, **1 tbsp creamed coconut (approximately 25g)** and **100ml more cold water**. Place over a low heat and cook, stirring frequently, for 5 minutes or until the porridge has thickened. Serve sprinkled with **a pinch of ground ginger**.

v

Nutty granola with mixed seeds

I love waking up to crunchy, home-made granola sprinkled over creamy yogurt or served with plenty of cold milk. This version has plenty of healthy nuts and seeds, as well as sweet dried apricots and chewy oat and barley flakes. Instant happiness.

15 minutes to prepare | 20–25 minutes active cooking | Makes 30 servings

150g clear honey

100g coconut oil

200g porridge oats

200g barley flakes

100g blanched almonds, roughly chopped

100g walnut pieces

50g pumpkin seeds

50g sunflower seeds

25g milled flaxseed

250g soft, dried, ready-to-eat apricots, chopped

1 Preheat the oven to gas mark 4/180°C/fan oven 160°C. Heat the honey and coconut oil together in a large pan until just melted. Stir in the oats and barley. Once they're coated, spread the grains out on 1 large or 2 medium baking trays and bake for 15–20 minutes, stirring 2–3 times to turn the grains, until golden brown.

2 Meanwhile, place a large frying pan over a low heat and dry fry the almonds, stirring occasionally, for 2–3 minutes or until golden and toasted. Tip into a bowl. Dry fry the walnuts for 2–3 minutes, stirring occasionally, then add to the almonds. Dry fry the pumpkin seeds for 1–2 minutes, stirring, until they crackle and add them to the nuts. Then dry fry the sunflower seeds for 1 minute, stirring, until toasted. Add to the nuts and pumpkin seeds.

3 Tip the cooked oats and barley into a very large mixing bowl. Stir in the toasted nuts and seeds, the milled flaxseed and the chopped apricots. Stir to mix and then store in an airtight container. A serving is approximately 30g.

🍳 KITCHEN TIP

The recipe multiplies really easily if you want to make extra for your family.

⏰ GET AHEAD >>
The granola will keep for 5–6 weeks in an airtight container, so it's perfect for making in the weeks before your due date.

V ⊛

millet porridge

If you're looking for a gluten-free alternative to oats for your morning porridge, try millet. It makes a soft, smooth porridge that I like topped with cinnamon, honey and yogurt.

2 minutes to prepare | 5–10 minutes active cooking | Makes 1 serving

40g millet flakes

6 tbsp cold water

100ml whole milk

1 tbsp natural yogurt

1 tsp clear honey

2 tsp pumpkin seeds

Ground cinnamon

1 Soak the millet overnight in the water. In the morning, tip the millet and any remaining water into a small pan. Add the milk and place the pan over a medium heat.

2 Bring to a simmer, then reduce the heat and cook gently, stirring frequently, for 5–10 minutes or until the porridge has thickened.

3 Spoon into a small bowl and top with the yogurt, honey and pumpkin seeds. Sprinkle over a pinch of ground cinnamon to serve.

V 🥕 ❄️

multiseed bread

Based on a recipe from Ballymaloe, this is a really easy bread that's perfect for first-time bakers. No kneading or proving – just mix it all together, let the loaves rise and then bake.

20 minutes to prepare + rising | 55–65 minutes total cooking time | Makes 2 loaves

Sunflower or olive oil, for greasing

600g strong wholemeal flour

200g strong white flour

2 x 7g sachets easy blend, fast action yeast

3 tbsp sunflower seeds

4 tbsp pumpkin seeds

2 tbsp milled flaxseed

2½ tsp salt

1 tbsp black treacle

750ml hand-hot water

2 tsp sesame seeds

2 tsp poppy seeds

1 Brush 2 loaf tins (approximately 20cm x 9cm) with oil so the sides and bottom are coated in a fine film of oil. Set aside.

2 Sift the flours into a large mixing bowl and tip in any bran that gets caught in the sieve. Add the yeast, sunflower seeds, pumpkin seeds, flaxseed and the salt and mix well with your hand. Add the treacle (warm the spoon under running hot water first to help the treacle slide off), then pour in all the warm water and stir together with your hand. The mixture should be wet and sloppy – too wet to knead.

3 Spoon the mixture into the loaf tins. Loosely cover with clingfilm or pop into carrier bags and leave somewhere warm for 20–30 minutes or until the dough has just come to the top of the tins.

4 Meanwhile, preheat the oven to gas mark 9/240°C/fan oven 220°C.

5 When the dough has risen, sprinkle the sesame and poppy seeds over the top. Bake the loaves for 15 minutes, then reduce the oven temperature to gas mark 6/200°C/fan oven 180°C and bake for a further 40–50 minutes or until the loaves feel light when they're tipped from the tin and the bottoms sound hollow when tapped. Cool on wire racks. The bread will keep well for 2–3 days.

⏱ GET AHEAD >>
This bread freezes brilliantly. Cut into slices, open freeze on a tray (to stop the slices sticking together) and then store in freezer bags. You can toast it from frozen.

4
toast toppers

Toast makes a quick and easy breakfast and there are lots of lactogenic toppings to choose from.

Pick one of our quick fixes or have a go at making a scrumptious nut or cinnamon butter and you'll always have something delicious to spread on your morning slice.

V 🥕 ⊛ ❄

1 Roasted almond butter

10 minutes to prepare | 5–8 minutes active cooking | Makes approximately 200g

Preheat the oven to gas mark 4/180°C/fan oven 160°C. Spread **200g whole almonds** on a baking tray and roast for 5–8 minutes, shaking the tray occasionally, until golden. Tip the almonds into a food processor and turn it on to a constant speed. After 3–4 minutes the almonds will turn to dust and then start to clump together. When this happens, add **2 tbsp virgin olive oil** and **a pinch of salt**. Process for another 3–4 minutes or until the almonds form a creamy butter. Spoon into a sterilised, airtight container or jar and store in the fridge for up to 1 month or freeze for up to 3 months.

V 🥕 ⊛ ❄

2 Sweet pecan butter

10 minutes to prepare | 5–8 minutes active cooking | Makes approximately 200g

Preheat the oven to gas mark 4/180°C/fan oven 160°C. Spread **150g pecan halves** on a baking tray and roast for 5–8 minutes, shaking the tray occasionally, until they smell sweet and nutty. Tip the pecans into a food processor and turn it on to a constant speed. Process for 2–3 minutes. The pecans will turn to dust and then start to clump together. When they start to clump, add **4 tbsp sunflower oil**, **1 tsp vanilla extract** and **3 tbsp caster sugar**. Process for 5–6 minutes or until it forms a creamy butter. Spoon into a sterilised, airtight jar and store in the fridge for up to 1 month or freeze for up to 3 months.

QUICK FIXES

- Butter and honey
- Tahini and sesame seeds
- Soft cheese, honey and sunflower seeds
- Eggs – poached, scrambled or fried
- Cheese and mango chutney
- Soft goat's cheese
- Jams with a high fruit content – apricot, cherry, peach or plum
- Smoked salmon and soft cheese

3 Chunky cashew nut butter

15 minutes to prepare | 8–10 minutes active cooking
Makes approximately 200g

Preheat the oven to gas mark 4/180°C/fan oven 160°C. Spread **200g cashew nuts** on a baking tray and roast for 8–10 minutes, shaking the tray occasionally, until golden and toasted. Tip ¾ of the cashews into a food processor with **a pinch of salt** and turn it on to a constant speed. Process for 3–4 minutes or until the cashews start to clump together. Add the remaining cashews to the processor with **3 tbsp virgin olive oil** and continue to process for 2–3 minutes or until it forms a creamy butter. Spoon into a sterilised, airtight container or jar and store in the fridge for up to 1 month or freeze for up to 3 months.

4 Quick cinnamon butter

5 minutes to prepare | Makes approximately 150g

Beat **125g room temperature butter** until it's soft and creamy. Beat in **2 tbsp caster sugar**, **2 tsp ground cinnamon** and **½ tsp ground ginger**. Spoon into a sterilised, airtight container or jar and store in the fridge for up to 1 month or freeze for up to 3 months.

V ❄

Fig and fennel scones

These scones will be a big hit at your breakfast table –
they're delicious warm from the oven, but they also freeze
well if you can resist the temptation to get stuck straight in.

25 minutes to prepare | 15–20 minutes total cooking time | Makes 8–10

450g plain flour,
plus extra for dusting

1 level tsp bicarbonate
of soda

1 tbsp caster sugar

2 tsp fennel seeds

150g soft, dried,
ready-to-eat figs

350ml whole milk
plus extra for glazing

Juice of ½ lemon

1 Preheat the oven to gas mark 7/220°C/fan oven 200°C. Sift the flour, soda and sugar into a large mixing bowl and stir in the fennel seeds and chopped figs.

2 Curdle the milk by stirring in the lemon juice. Add 300ml of the curdled milk to the flour, stirring it in with your hand. If the dough is still dry and floury, add the remaining milk – you may not need all the milk or may you need to add a little extra – to make a soft but not sticky dough.

3 Working quickly, dust your work surface with flour and turn out the dough. Pat into a 3cm high round and stamp out scones with a 6½cm round cutter. Repeat with any remaining dough until you have 8–10 scones. Place the scones on a baking tray and brush with milk to glaze.

4 Bake for 15–20 minutes or until they're golden and cooked through. Cool for a few minutes on a wire rack and then serve with butter and jam.

🍳 KITCHEN TIP

Measure the bicarbonate with a normal teaspoon.
If you're using a measuring spoon, use the ½ teaspoon measure.

⏰ **GET AHEAD >>**
You can freeze these scones in freezer bags for up to 3 months. To reheat, defrost overnight and then warm through at gas mark 3/170°C/fan oven 150°C for 10–15 minutes.

V ❄

Sweet potato and pecan muffins

These American-style muffins are out of this world eaten warm, but the sweet potato, carrots, almonds and pecans keep them nice and moist, so they'll last a few days in your bread bin.

25 minutes to prepare | 20–25 minutes total cooking time | Makes 12

2 medium eggs

50g caster sugar

100ml sunflower oil

250g sweet potato, peeled and coarsely grated

150g carrots, peeled and coarsely grated

150g self-raising flour

2 tsp baking powder

1 tsp bicarbonate of soda

2 tsp ground cinnamon

100g ground almonds

100g pecans, roughly chopped

1 Preheat the oven to gas mark 4/180°C/fan oven 160°C. Line 2 x 6-hole muffin tins with paper muffin cases.

2 Whisk the eggs, sugar and oil together in a large bowl until pale and combined. Stir in the sweet potato and carrots.

3 Sift the flour, baking powder, bicarbonate of soda and cinnamon into a separate bowl. Stir in the ground almonds and pecans.

4 Quickly stir the dry ingredients into the wet ingredients – don't over stir the mixture. A few floury lumps are fine. Spoon the muffin mixture into the muffin cases and bake for 20–25 minutes or until risen, golden and springy to the touch. Cool the muffins on a wire rack for a few minutes before serving.

⏰ GET AHEAD >>
These muffins will keep for up to 3 days or they can be frozen for up to 3 months. Defrost overnight and warm through in an oven at gas mark 3/170°C/fan oven 150°C for about 10 minutes.

V 🥕 ⊛

Papaya, mango and coconut salad

A fresh fruit salad that's full of tropical flavours,
this makes a light and refreshing breakfast.

20 minutes to prepare + chilling | Makes 2 servings

300g papaya

1 large mango

30g dried,
pitted dates
roughly chopped

Zest of 2 limes

10g desiccated
coconut

1 Peel, halve and deseed the papaya. Chop into bite-size chunks and place in a large bowl.

2 Cut the 2 fat cheeks off the mango, as close to the stone as possible. Score a criss-cross pattern in the mango flesh close to the skin, but not cutting all the way through. Push the skin up to turn the mango cheeks inside out, making a hedgehog.

3 Run a knife along the skin to separate off the mango chunks and add these to the papaya. Slice the remaining mango off the stone. Slice off the skin, chop the flesh and add to the papaya.

4 Add the dates, lime zest and desiccated coconut and stir to mix. Tip into a bowl or tub, cover and chill overnight before serving.

⏰ GET AHEAD >>

This fruit salad can be served straight away but it tastes even better if it's left to chill overnight and it will keep for up to 2 days.

V Ⓥ

Vanilla and star anise poached plums

A decadent breakfast, these spicy poached plums
are also good served up as dessert.

10 minutes to prepare | 10–15 minutes active cooking time | Makes 4 servings

8 plums, stoned
and quartered

30g caster sugar

1 star anise

Freshly ground
black pepper

1 vanilla pod

Natural yogurt,
to serve

1 Place the plums and sugar in a small pan with the star anise and a large
pinch of freshly ground black pepper. Split the vanilla pod open and scrape
out the seeds. Add the seeds and the pod to the plums with 4 tbsp water.

2 Place over a medium heat, cover and bring to a gentle simmer. Reduce
the heat and gently cook for 5–10 minutes or until the plums are tender.
Remove the vanilla pod and star anise and discard.

3 Serve the poached plums warm or cold with natural yogurt.

🍳 KITCHEN TIP

The vanilla pod halves can be washed, dried and added to a bag
of sugar to make vanilla flavoured sugar for baking and sprinkling.

⏰ **GET AHEAD >>**
The poached plums
will keep in an airtight
container in the fridge
for up to 5 days.

Light lunches

A quick bite – soup, sandwich or salad –
keeps me going during the day and I especially
love the Thai chicken soup on page 35
when I need a pick-me-up.

5
ways with chicken soup

Is there anything more homely and comforting than chicken soup? We've come up with 5 different versions, from traditional to Thai, and an easy stock recipe so you can cook your soup from scratch.

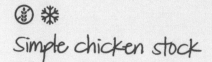

Simple chicken stock

15 minutes to prepare | 1 hour total cooking time | Makes approximately 1½ litres

Place **3 chicken drumsticks**, **3 chicken thighs**, **1 onion**, halved, **1 carrot** and **1 stick celery**, both roughly chopped, in a large pan with **1½ litres cold water**. Cover, bring to the boil and then reduce the heat. Simmer, covered, for 45 minutes. Pour the stock through a heatproof sieve into a large bowl or jug. When the chicken is cool enough to handle, pull the meat from the bones. Discard the skin, bones and vegetables. You can use the stock straight away or cool and stir in the chicken meat. It will keep for 3 days in the fridge (you can skim off the fat before using) or freeze it for up to 3 months.

3 Chicken and barley

20 minutes to prepare | 25 minutes active cooking | 50 minutes total cooking time | Makes 6 servings

Melt **25g butter** in a large pan and add **2 onions**, finely chopped. Season, cover with a piece of greaseproof paper and the pan lid and sweat over a low heat for 10 minutes, stirring occasionally. Add **3 sticks celery**, chopped, and **3 medium carrots**, peeled and sliced. Re-cover and sweat for 5 minutes. Discard the greaseproof paper. Add **1½ litres chicken stock** and the **chicken** to the pan with **75g pearl barley** and **3 sprigs rosemary**. Cover, bring to the boil and then gently simmer for 45 minutes, adding **600g potatoes**, peeled and chopped, for the final 20 minutes. Lift out the rosemary sprigs, season to taste and serve.

1 Garlicky chicken and mushroom

20 minutes to prepare | 25 minutes active cooking
| 50 minutes total cooking time | Makes 6 servings

Melt **25g butter** in a large pan and add **2 onions**, finely chopped. Season, cover with a piece of greaseproof paper and the pan lid and sweat over a low heat for 10 minutes, stirring occasionally. Discard the greaseproof paper. Stir in **2 cloves garlic**, crushed, and **400g closed cap mushrooms**, sliced, and fry, stirring frequently, for 15 minutes. Add **1½ litres chicken stock** and the **chicken** with **6 sprigs fresh thyme**. Cover, bring to a boil, then reduce the heat and simmer for 20 minutes. Lift out the thyme, stir in **200ml whole milk** and ladle into a blender. Blitz until smooth. Taste, season and serve.

🍳 KITCHEN TIP

If you're freezing this soup, blitz it without adding the milk and freeze. Add the milk when you reheat it.

2 Chicken and sweet potato

15–20 minutes to prepare | 10 minutes active cooking
| 30–35 minutes total cooking time | Makes 4 servings

Melt **1 tbsp coconut oil** in a large pan and add **10 spring onions**, sliced. Season, cover with a sheet of greaseproof paper and the pan lid and sweat over a low heat for 5 minutes, stirring occasionally. Add **2 cloves garlic**, crushed, **30g fresh ginger**, peeled and grated, **1 tsp each ground allspice** and **cinnamon**, **½ tsp chilli powder** and **a pinch of freshly grated nutmeg**. Re-cover with the greaseproof paper and pan lid and sweat for a further 5 minutes. Discard the greaseproof paper. Stir in **1½ litres chicken stock** and the **chicken**, **1 x 400g can kidney beans**, drained, **2 tsp muscovado sugar** and **3–4 sprigs fresh thyme**. Cover and bring to the boil. Add **500g sweet potatoes**, peeled and chopped, and simmer for 10–15 minutes. Discard the thyme. Stir in **50g spinach**, season and serve.

4 Thai coconut and chicken

15 minutes to prepare | 6 minutes active cooking
| 45 minutes total cooking time | Makes 6 servings

Melt **½ tbsp coconut oil** in a pan and add **6 shallots**, peeled and sliced. Fry, stirring, over a low heat for 5 minutes or until starting to soften. Add **1 stick lemongrass**, **2 cloves garlic**, crushed, **30g fresh ginger**, peeled and grated, **1 red chilli**, finely chopped, and the grated zest of **1 lime**. Fry, stirring, for 1 minute, then add **1½ litres chicken stock** and the **chicken**, **1 x 400ml can coconut milk**, **3 tsp Thai fish sauce**, **4 tsp soy sauce**, **1 red pepper**, deseeded and finely chopped, and **200g frozen peas**. Season with a pinch of salt and bring to the boil. Reduce the heat and simmer for 10 minutes. Fish out the lemongrass, stir in a handful of **fresh coriander leaves** and serve.

5 Chicken, chickpea and kale

15 minutes to prepare | 20 minutes active cooking
| 45–50 minutes total cooking time | Makes 4 servings

Warm **1 tbsp olive oil** in a large pan and add **1 onion**, finely chopped. Season, cover with a sheet of greaseproof paper and the pan lid and sweat over a low heat for 10 minutes, stirring occasionally. Add **2 sticks celery**, chopped, and **2 medium carrots**, peeled and chopped, re-cover and sweat for a further 5 minutes. Discard the greaseproof paper. Stir in **1 tsp ground cumin** and **½ tsp paprika**, then add **1½ litres chicken stock** and the **chicken**, **1 x 410g can cooked chickpeas**, drained, and **1 x 400g can chopped tomatoes**. Cover, bring to the boil, then reduce the heat and simmer for 20 minutes. Add **150g kale** or **Savoy cabbage**, shredded, and cook for a further 5 minutes. Season to taste and serve.

⏰ GET AHEAD >>

All the soups can be frozen for up to 3 months.

V 🥕 ❄

Vegetable barley soup

This chunky, farmhouse-style soup is perfect for warming up cold days and you can swap or add in vegetables depending on what's in season. Asparagus, peas, broad beans, sliced runner or French beans, broccoli florets, chard and spinach would all be tasty, lactogenic additions.

15 minutes to prepare | 15 minutes active cooking | 50 minutes total cooking time | Makes 4 servings

1 tbsp sunflower oil

1 onion, chopped

1 small leek, trimmed and sliced

1 clove garlic, crushed

3 sticks celery, chopped

3 medium carrots, peeled and chopped

1 medium parsnip, peeled and chopped

100g pearl barley, rinsed

1¼ litres hot vegetable stock

100g kale or Savoy cabbage, shredded

Crusty bread, to serve

1 Warm the oil in a large pan. Stir in the onion, leek, garlic, celery, carrots and parsnip and season with salt and freshly ground black pepper. Cover with a piece of greaseproof paper and the pan lid. Sweat over a very low heat for 15 minutes, stirring once or twice, or until softened.

2 Discard the greaseproof paper. Add the pearl barley and vegetable stock. Cover and bring to the boil. Reduce the heat and simmer for 30 minutes or until the barley is tender.

3 Add the kale or cabbage and simmer, uncovered, for 1–2 minutes. Taste and adjust the seasoning, then ladle into warm bowls and serve with crusty bread.

⏰ **GET AHEAD >>**
Cool the soup and ladle into tubs or soup bags and freeze for up to 3 months. To reheat, defrost overnight and warm through in a pan with a splash of extra water or stock, if necessary.

V 🥕 ⊘ ❄

Pea and coconut soup with chilli and lemongrass

This spicy soup has plenty of fragrant flavours. Reduce the chilli or leave it out entirely if you prefer your meals a bit milder.

25–30 minutes to prepare | 25 minutes active cooking | 40–50 minutes total cooking time | Makes 6 servings

2 tbsp coconut oil

1 onion, finely chopped

4 cloves garlic, crushed

1–2 tsp dried
red chilli flakes

2 stalks lemongrass,
roughly chopped

200g potatoes, peeled
and diced

900g peas,
defrosted if frozen

1 litre hot vegetable stock

400ml coconut milk

1 bunch fresh
coriander leaves

1 Add the coconut oil to a large pan and place over a very low heat. Add the onion and stir to coat in the oil. Season with a little salt and freshly ground black pepper, then cover with a piece of greaseproof paper and the pan lid. Sweat the onion over a very low heat for 10 minutes, stirring 2–3 times to make sure it doesn't catch or colour.

2 Stir the garlic, chilli flakes, lemongrass and potatoes into the onions. Season again, re-cover with the greaseproof paper and the pan lid and sweat for 10 more minutes, stirring once or twice, or until the potatoes are starting to soften.

3 Discard the greaseproof paper. Add the peas, stock and coconut milk. Turn up the heat and bring to a gentle boil, uncovered. Reduce the heat and simmer for 10 minutes, until the vegetables are tender. Stir in the coriander leaves.

4 Ladle the soup, in batches, into a blender and blitz until smooth. Pour the blitzed soup through a sieve into a large bowl to catch any unblended bits. Press the fibrous vegetable matter in the sieve to squeeze out as much soup as possible. Taste, adjust the seasoning and serve.

⏰ GET AHEAD >>

To freeze the soup, let it cool down and then ladle into airtight containers or sealable freezerproof bags. This soup will keep in the freezer for up to 3 months. Defrost overnight and warm through over a medium heat to serve.

V 🌾 ❄️

Fennel and spinach soup

Sweating the vegetables over a low heat before you add the stock means they cook without you having to stand over the pan, stirring them constantly. Make sure you keep the lid off once you add the spinach – cooking green vegetables with the lid on turns them grey.

25 minutes to prepare | 20 minutes active cooking | 40 minutes total cooking time | Makes 4 servings

25g butter

1 onion,
finely chopped

200g potatoes,
peeled and diced

750g fennel bulbs,
trimmed and
finely chopped

1¼ litres hot
vegetable stock

100g baby leaf spinach

1 Melt the butter in a large pan. Stir in the onion and season with salt and freshly ground black pepper. Cover with a piece of greaseproof paper and the pan lid. Sweat the onion over a very low heat for 10 minutes, stirring once or twice, or until the onion has softened.

2 Stir in the potatoes and fennel. Season again, re-cover with the greaseproof paper and pan lid and continue to sweat for 10 minutes, stirring once or twice, or until the potatoes have softened.

3 Discard the greaseproof paper. Add the stock and bring to a gentle boil. Reduce the heat and simmer for 15 minutes, until the vegetables are tender. Remove the lid and stir in the spinach so it wilts.

4 Ladle the soup, in batches, into a blender and blitz until smooth. Taste and adjust the seasoning, if necessary, then ladle into bowls and serve.

⏰ GET AHEAD >>

Let the soup cool and freeze for up to 3 months. To reheat, defrost overnight and then warm through, uncovered, with an extra splash of stock if necessary.

Grilled prawns with fennel slaw

Prepare this crunchy coleslaw and marinate the prawns the night before when – if! – you have a quiet moment and in 10 minutes you can have a stylish lunch ready the next day.

20 minutes to prepare + marinating | 8–10 minutes active cooking time | Makes 2 servings

200g raw,
shelled king prawns

2 tbsp olive oil

1 clove garlic crushed

150g fennel bulb

100g red cabbage

100g carrot

A small handful
of fresh dill

1 tsp fennel seeds

½ tbsp white
wine vinegar

1 tsp clear honey

Crusty bread, to serve

1 Place the prawns in a bowl with 1 tbsp of the olive oil and the garlic. Season with freshly ground black pepper and toss to coat in the oil. Set aside to marinate for 30 minutes or overnight in the fridge.

2 Meanwhile, trim and finely slice the fennel bulb and shred the red cabbage. Peel and coarsely grate the carrot and roughly chop the dill. Place the vegetables and dill in a bowl with the fennel seeds and toss to mix.

3 Preheat the grill to high and line the grill pan with foil.

4 Whisk the remaining olive oil, the white wine vinegar and honey with a pinch of salt and black pepper until opaque and emulsified. Drizzle over the vegetables and toss to lightly coat them. Arrange the fennel slaw on 2 serving plates and set aside.

5 Thread the prawns onto small skewers and grill for 8–10 minutes, turning once, until cooked through. Serve the prawn skewers with the slaw and crusty bread.

⏰ GET AHEAD >>
The slaw will keep in the fridge for 2–3 days and the cooked prawns are good cold as well as hot, so you can make this a day ahead or save a portion for later.

V Ⓥ

warm roast vegetable and goat's cheese salad

Pack plenty of veg into just one meal with this hearty salad. Chop the vegetables and toss them with the oil and garlic the night before to save time during the day.

20 minutes to prepare | 10 minutes active cooking | 30 minutes total cooking time | Makes 2 servings

1 medium courgette

1 medium aubergine

1 red pepper, halved and deseeded

1 red onion, sliced into thin wedges

2 cloves garlic, crushed

2 tbsp extra virgin olive oil

Small bunch of fresh basil leaves, torn

100g quinoa, rinsed

300ml just boiled water

50g firm goat's cheese, chopped

2 tsp sunflower seeds

Mustard dressing

2 tbsp extra virgin olive oil

1 tbsp white wine vinegar

1 tsp Dijon mustard

A pinch of caster sugar

1 Preheat the oven to gas mark 9/240°C/fan oven 220°C.

2 Chop the courgette, aubergine and pepper into chunks about 2cm square. Place them in a bowl with the onion, garlic, oil and most of the basil leaves. Season and toss to coat the vegetables in the oil. Tip them into a roasting tin, spreading them out, and roast for 30 minutes or until the vegetables are tender and starting to char.

3 Meanwhile, place the quinoa in a pan with the water and a pinch of salt. Cover and gently simmer for 10 minutes or until almost all the water has been absorbed. Remove from the heat and leave to steam for a further 10 minutes, then stir to separate the grains.

4 Spoon the quinoa into 2 shallow bowls. Top with the roasted vegetables, the goat's cheese, the remaining basil leaves and the sunflower seeds.

5 Whisk the oil, vinegar, Dijon mustard and sugar together and season. Drizzle over the salad and serve.

⏰ **GET AHEAD >>**
This salad is good eaten warm from the oven or cold the next day. Store, covered, in the fridge and eat within 2–3 days.

V 🥕

Quick chickpea and couscous salad

Super speedy and easy to put together, this Sicilian salad is great as it is or as a side dish with grilled fish or meat.

15 minutes to prepare | Makes 2 servings

80g couscous

175ml just boiled water

1 x 410g can chickpeas, drained and rinsed

½ medium red onion, finely chopped

1 clove garlic, finely chopped

A pinch of dried chilli flakes

Large handful of fresh coriander or basil leaves, chopped

2 tbsp extra virgin olive oil

1½ tbsp red or white wine vinegar

1 Place the couscous in a heatproof bowl and cover with the water. Cover with clingfilm or a saucer and set aside for 10 minutes or until the water has all been absorbed.

2 Meanwhile, mix together the chickpeas, red onion, garlic, chilli flakes and coriander or basil leaves. Whisk the olive oil and vinegar together with a pinch of salt and freshly ground black pepper until opaque and emulsified. Pour over the chickpeas and toss to coat.

3 Fluff up the couscous with a fork and stir into the chickpeas. Divide between 2 plates to serve.

⏰ GET AHEAD >>

The chickpea salad will keep in the fridge, covered, for 3–4 days but it does get garlickier the longer it sits. If you plan to keep it for a couple of days, leave out the garlic and add a small crushed clove per portion just before serving.

6
sandwich fillings

Fast food doesn't come much quicker than sandwiches and these filling ideas will keep lunchtime interesting as well as help you include tasty, lactogenic foods in your meals.

V

1 Cheddar and coleslaw

10 minutes to prepare | Makes 1 serving

Combine **4 Little Gem lettuce leaves**, shredded, **1 small carrot**, peeled and coarsely grated, **1 spring onion**, finely shredded, **2 tbsp natural yogurt** and **1 tsp wholegrain mustard** together to make a creamy coleslaw. Season. Heap over **a slice of bread**, top with some **slices of mature Cheddar cheese** and cover with another **slice of bread** to serve.

⏰ GET AHEAD >>

The coleslaw will keep for 1–2 days in an airtight container in the fridge and it's also good with sliced roast turkey or chicken breast.

4 Mackerel, soft cheese and beetroot

5 minutes to prepare | Makes 1 serving

Spread **a slice of bread** with **30g soft cheese** and top with **50g smoked mackerel**, flaked, **1 small cooked beetroot** (not stored in vinegar), drained and sliced, and sprinkle over **1 tbsp fresh dill**, chopped. Season with freshly ground black pepper, cover with another **slice of bread** and serve.

2 Houmous, carrot and sesame seed

15 minutes to prepare | Makes 1 serving + extra houmous

Make the houmous by placing **1 x 410g can chickpeas**, drained and rinsed, **1 clove garlic**, crushed, the juice of **½ lemon**, **6 tbsp extra virgin olive oil**, **2 tbsp tahini paste** and **a pinch of salt** into a food processor and blitz to make a smooth paste. Taste and season with salt and more lemon juice or olive oil if you think it's necessary.

To make the sandwich, dollop a few spoonfuls of the houmous onto **a slice of bread** and top with **1 small carrot**, peeled and grated, and **1 tsp sesame seeds**. Season and cover with another **slice of bread** to serve.

⏰ GET AHEAD >>

This recipe makes around 4–5 servings of houmous. It'll keep in the fridge for about a week or can be frozen for 3–4 weeks.

3 Turkey, mozzarella and tomato

5 minutes to prepare | Makes 1 serving

Spread **2 slices of bread** with **2 tsp pesto**. Top the bottom slice with **60g mozzarella**, drained and sliced, **2 slices roast turkey breast**, **1 tomato**, sliced, and **a few fresh basil leaves.** Season with black pepper and cover with the remaining **slice of bread** to serve.

🧑‍🍳 **KITCHEN TIP**

This sandwich is also good hot – assemble the sandwich, place on a baking tray, brush with olive oil and bake for 20 minutes at gas mark 5/ 190°C/fan oven 170°C or grill, turning once, for 5 minutes.

5 Smoked salmon and egg

10 minutes to prepare | 10 minutes total cooking time | Makes 1 serving

Cook **1 egg** in boiling water for 10 minutes, then transfer to a bowl of cold water to cool. When it's cool enough to handle, peel and slice. Spread **1½ tsp Dijon mustard** over **2 slices of bread** and arrange **3–4 cornichons**, sliced, over the bottom slice. Top with **a handful of rocket**, the egg and **20g smoked salmon trimmings**. Season with black pepper. Cover with the remaining slice of bread to serve.

6 Artichoke, pepper and goat's cheese

5 minutes to prepare | Makes 1 serving

Spread **50g soft goat's cheese** over **2 slices of bread,** then top the bottom slice with **30g artichoke in oil**, drained, **50g roasted red peppers in brine and vinegar**, drained and torn, and a **handful of baby leaf spinach**. Season with black pepper and cover with the remaining slice of bread to serve.

Main meals

A freezer full of delicious, home-made meals makes those first weeks and months after your baby is born that bit easier. There are lots of options here, so there'll be something to tickle your fancy every night of the week.

❄

Spaghetti bolognese

I've given this family favourite a boost by adding lactogenic
vegetables to the sauce – it's a big hit with all ages.

15–20 minutes to prepare | 30 minutes active cooking | 1 hour 15–20 minutes total cooking time
| Makes 4 servings

1 tbsp extra virgin olive oil

1 onion, finely chopped

2 cloves garlic

2 sticks celery

2 medium carrots, peeled

100g mushrooms, cleaned

1 medium courgette

400g lean steak mince

1 x 400g can
chopped tomatoes

2 tbsp tomato purée

300ml hot vegetable stock

1 bay leaf

2 tsp fresh marjoram leaves
or 1 tsp dried marjoram

450g dried spaghetti

Parmesan cheese, to serve

1 Warm the olive oil in a pan over a very low heat and stir in the onion. Season, cover with a piece of greaseproof paper and the pan lid and leave to sweat for 15 minutes, stirring occasionally so it doesn't stick.

2 While the onion is sweating, peel and crush the garlic and finely chop the celery, carrots, mushrooms and courgette.

3 Discard the paper and stir in the chopped vegetables. Season and fry over a medium heat, stirring frequently, for 10 minutes or until the veg have softened and any liquid has evaporated.

4 Stir in the steak mince, breaking up any lumps, then stir in the chopped tomatoes, tomato purée and vegetable stock. Add the bay leaf and marjoram, cover and bring to a simmer. Simmer for 45–50 minutes, stirring occasionally, until the sauce has thickened. Remove the bay leaf. Taste and adjust the seasoning, if necessary.

5 Cook the spaghetti according to the packet instructions in a large pan of salted water. Drain and divide between 4 warm serving plates. Top with the bolognese sauce and serve with finely grated Parmesan cheese.

⏰ **GET AHEAD >>**
You can freeze the bolognese sauce for up to 3 months. Just cool and spoon into freezerproof containers or soup bags. Defrost overnight and reheat.

V ❄

Spinach and mushroom pasta bake

This is a souped-up version of macaroni cheese with earthy spinach and mushroom adding plenty of flavour.

20 minutes to prepare | 35 minutes active cooking | 55 minutes–1 hour total cooking time | Makes 4 servings

300g dried
macaroni pasta

200g spinach

55g butter

250g closed cap
mushrooms, sliced

40g plain flour

700ml whole milk

1 tsp Dijon mustard

175g mature Cheddar
cheese, grated

Freshly grated nutmeg,
to season

1 Preheat the oven to gas mark 5/190°C/fan oven 170°C.

2 Add the macaroni to a large pan of salted boiling water and cook for 5 minutes. Drain and return to the pan. Stir in the spinach and set aside.

3 Meanwhile, melt 15g of the butter in a large frying pan and add the mushrooms. Season with a pinch of salt and black pepper and fry over a medium heat, stirring frequently, for 10 minutes or until tender and any liquid has evaporated. Stir into the macaroni.

4 Melt the remaining butter in a small pan and whisk in the flour. Cook, whisking constantly, over a low heat for 2 minutes, then slowly whisk in the milk, a little at a time, until it's smoothly combined with the roux (flour and butter mixture).

5 Bring the sauce to the boil, whisking constantly, then simmer, whisking frequently, for 15 minutes or until the sauce has thickened. Stir in the mustard and ¾ of the Cheddar. Season to taste with nutmeg, salt and freshly ground black pepper.

6 Stir the cheese sauce into the macaroni and then spoon into 4 x 400ml ovenproof and freezerproof dishes. Sprinkle over the remaining Cheddar and bake for 20–25 minutes or until golden and bubbling. Leave to cool for 5–10 minutes before serving.

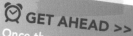

⏰ GET AHEAD >>
Once the pasta bake is assembled, you can cool it and freeze it for up to 3 months. Cook from frozen at gas mark 5/190°C/fan oven 170°C for 45 minutes until golden, bubbling and hot all the way through.

V ❄

Butternut squash and kale lasagne

The perfect dish when a crowd of well-wishers decide to visit!

30 minutes to prepare + infusing | 30 minutes active cooking | 1 hour 30 minutes total cooking time | Makes 6 servings

1½ kg butternut squash, peeled, deseeded and chopped into bite-sized chunks

½ tbsp extra virgin olive oil

1 litre whole milk

1 small onion, peeled

½ small bunch fresh sage

40g butter

40g plain flour

200g kale, shredded and any woody bits removed

250g dried lasagne sheets

2 x 400g can chopped tomatoes with garlic and herbs

250g soft, medium fat goat's cheese, chopped

Rocket and watercress salad, to serve

1 Preheat the oven to gas mark 8/230°C/fan oven 210°C. Toss the chopped butternut squash with the oil and some salt and freshly ground black pepper, then spread out on a baking tray. Roast for 30 minutes or until tender.

2 Meanwhile, place the milk, onion and sage in a pan, cover and bring to the boil. Remove from the heat and set aside to infuse for 15 minutes.

3 Strain the infused milk through a sieve and discard the onion and sage. Melt the butter in a pan and whisk in the flour. Cook, whisking, for 2 minutes, then slowly whisk in the milk until it's combined to make a smooth sauce. Bring to the boil, then reduce the heat and simmer, whisking constantly, for 10 minutes or until the béchamel sauce has just thickened. Remove from the heat and stir in the kale. Season.

4 Spread 1–2 tbsp of the béchamel over the base of a 2 litre ovenproof dish and cover with ⅓ of the lasagne. Top with ½ the roasted butternut squash, ½ the tomatoes and ⅓ of the remaining béchamel. Season and sprinkle over ⅓ of the goat's cheese.

5 Arrange another ⅓ of the lasagne in the dish and cover with the remaining butternut squash and tomatoes, ⅓ of the béchamel and ⅓ of the goat's cheese. Season.

6 Cover with a final layer of lasagne sheets, pour over the remaining béchamel and top with the remaining goat's cheese. Bake for 30 minutes or until the top is golden. Serve with a rocket and watercress salad.

⏰ GET AHEAD >>

The lasagne can be assembled up to 24 hours ahead and kept covered in the fridge, ready to bake. It will take 10–15 minutes longer to cook. Leftover cooked portions can be frozen in freezerproof containers for up to 3 months – defrost and reheat in the microwave. Alternatively, once the lasagne is assembled, wrap in freezer wrap and freeze for up to 3 months. Cook from frozen for 1 hour 30 minutes at gas mark 4/180°C/fan oven 160°C, covering the top with foil for the first 1 hour, then remove and cook uncovered until the lasagne is golden and cooked through.

V ✿

Oven-baked beetroot risotto

If you ever thought risotto was too much effort to make at home, this oven-baked version will make you think again. A few minutes stirring, then into the oven and it's done.

10 minutes to prepare | 8 minutes active cooking | 40 minutes total cooking time | Makes 4 servings

1 tbsp extra virgin olive oil

1 onion, finely chopped

300g dried risotto rice

250g cooked beetroot, not stored in vinegar, finely chopped

150ml white wine, such as Pinot Grigio

700ml hot vegetable stock

50g Parmesan cheese, finely grated

25g butter

1 tbsp fresh dill, roughly chopped

Green salad, to serve

1 Preheat the oven to gas mark 6/200°C/fan oven 180°C.

2 Warm the oil in an ovenproof casserole dish over a medium heat. Add the onion, season well, and fry, stirring frequently, for 5 minutes or until the onion has started to soften.

3 Stir in the rice and beetroot, then add the wine and cook, stirring, for 2–3 minutes or until the wine has been absorbed. Stir in the hot vegetable stock, cover with a tight fitting lid and bake in the oven for 30 minutes or until the rice is tender.

4 Stir in the Parmesan, butter and dill. Taste and adjust the seasoning, then serve on warm plates with a peppery green salad.

🍳 KITCHEN TIP

Leftover risotto can be shaped into rounds, dipped in flour and fried in a splash of olive oil, turning once, until crunchy and heated all the way through. Serve with salad and a poached egg.

❄

Beef stew and dumplings

When I want something hearty, I make stew and dumplings.

20 minutes to prepare | 15–20 minutes active cooking | 3 hours 50 minutes total cooking time | Makes 4 servings

1 tbsp extra virgin olive oil

1kg stewing steak, chopped

1 onion, roughly chopped

1 clove garlic, crushed

5 medium carrots, peeled and thickly sliced

300g turnips, peeled and roughly chopped

1 bay leaf

500ml bottle of ale, such as London Pride

700ml hot beef stock

Steamed kale, to serve

Dumplings:

150g self-raising flour

25g porridge oats

80g beef suet

1 Preheat the oven to gas mark 3/170°C/fan oven 150°C.

2 Heat the oil in an ovenproof casserole dish and add half the beef. Fry, stirring occasionally, for 3–4 minutes or until browned all over. Remove from the dish and set aside. Fry the remaining beef until browned, then remove from the pan and set aside.

3 Add the onion to the dish with a splash of water and season with salt and freshly ground black pepper. Fry, stirring, over a low heat for 3–4 minutes or until starting to soften and the water has evaporated. Add the garlic and fry for a further 2 minutes.

4 Return the beef to the pan with any juices and the carrots, turnips and bay. Season, pour in the beer and hot beef stock and bring to a simmer. Cover, transfer to the oven and cook for 3 hours.

5 After 3 hours, make the dumplings. Sift the flour into a large mixing bowl and mix in the oats and suet with a pinch of salt. Stir in enough cold water to make a thick dough. Shape into 4 large or 8 small dumplings and place on top of the stew straight away.

6 Cover and return to the oven for 30 more minutes. When the dumplings have doubled in size and are firm, the stew is ready. Discard the bay leaf, ladle the stew into warm bowls and serve with steamed kale.

⏰ GET AHEAD >>
Let the stew cool and then ladle it into freezerproof, microwaveproof containers. Defrost overnight and reheat in the microwave until piping hot.

Lamb and date tagine

This North African dish mixes sweet dried dates into a spicy lamb stew – delicious served with rice.

15 minutes to prepare + marinating | 20 minutes active cooking | 1 hour 50 minutes total cooking time | Makes 6 servings

700g lamb leg steak, chopped into bite-size chunks

1 tsp ground coriander

1 tsp ground cumin

1 tsp ground cinnamon

½ tsp chilli powder

½ tsp turmeric

20g fresh ginger, peeled and grated

4 cloves garlic, crushed

2 tbsp extra virgin olive oil

2 onions, roughly chopped

1 x 400g can chopped tomatoes

600ml hot chicken stock

200g dried, ready-to-eat, pitted dates

Grated zest and juice of 1 lemon (optional)

Cooked rice and green vegetables, to serve

1 Place the lamb in a non-metallic bowl with the dry spices, ½ tsp salt, the ginger and garlic. Turn to coat, cover and leave to marinate for 2 hours or overnight in the fridge.

2 Preheat the oven to gas mark 4/180°C/fan oven 160°C. Heat the oil in an ovenproof casserole dish over a medium heat. Add the onions, season and cook gently for 5 minutes or until starting to soften and brown.

3 Add the lamb and its spices and fry, stirring, for 10 minutes, or until the lamb is browned and aromatic.

4 Add the tomatoes, chicken stock, dates and lemon zest and juice, if using. Bring to the boil, then cover and transfer to the oven. Cook for 1 hour 30 minutes or until the lamb is very tender.

5 Serve the tagine with rice, cooked according to the packet instructions, and steamed green vegetables, such as kale or broccoli.

⏰ GET AHEAD >>
Cool the tagine and divide between freezerproof containers. The tagine will freeze for up to 3 months. To reheat, defrost overnight and heat in a pan with an extra splash of water or chicken stock until piping hot.

chicken, almond and apricot casserole

The warming spices and almond milk give this
chicken casserole a Middle Eastern twist.

15 minutes to prepare | 20–25 minutes active cooking | 1 hour 25 minutes total cooking time | Makes 4 servings

2 tbsp plain flour

1 tsp paprika

8 chicken thighs

2 tbsp extra virgin olive oil

2 onions, finely chopped

4 cloves garlic, crushed

25g fresh ginger,
peeled and grated

1 cinnamon stick

4 cardamom pods

¼ tsp ground cloves

½ tsp turmeric

Grated zest of 1 orange

200g dried,
ready-to-eat apricots

50g ground almonds

450ml almond milk

400ml hot chicken stock

Couscous or boiled
potatoes and green
vegetables, to serve

1 Preheat the oven to gas mark 4/180°C/fan oven 160°C. Sprinkle the
flour on a plate and season with salt, freshly ground black pepper and the
paprika. Roll the chicken thighs in the flour to coat, shaking off any excess.

2 Heat 1 tbsp of the oil in a casserole dish over a medium heat. Fry the chicken
thighs, in batches if necessary, turning occasionally until browned all over.
Remove from the pan and set aside.

3 Reduce the heat, add the remaining oil and fry the onions for 5 minutes,
stirring frequently, until starting to soften. Season and stir in the garlic,
ginger, cinnamon, cardamom, cloves, turmeric and orange zest and
cook for a further 1 minute.

4 Stir in the apricots and ground almonds, then return the chicken to the pan
with any juices and any remaining flour. Pour in the almond milk and chicken
stock. Bring to a simmer, then cover and transfer to the oven. Cook for 1 hour
or until the chicken is tender.

5 Taste and adjust the seasoning. Serve the chicken with couscous,
made up according to the packet instructions, or boiled potatoes
and steamed green vegetables.

⏰ GET AHEAD >>

Cool the casserole and divide between freezerproof containers.
The casserole will freeze for up to 3 months. Defrost overnight
and reheat in the microwave until piping hot.

V 🥕 🌾 ❄️

Tunisian chickpea and lentil stew

Harissa paste gives this spicy stew its heat. Swap it for ½–1 tsp dried chilli flakes and 1 tsp tomato purée if you can't get it in your local shops.

20 minutes to prepare + overnight soaking | 25 minutes active cooking
| 55 minutes total cooking time | Makes 4 servings

150g red lentils,
soaked overnight

2 tbsp extra
virgin olive oil

2 onions,
finely chopped

4 cloves garlic, crushed

40g coriander leaves
and stalks, chopped

2 x 410g cans
chickpeas, drained

6 tomatoes,
roughly chopped

1 tsp ground cumin

1–2 tsp harissa paste

900ml hot vegetable stock

75g green olives, pitted
and sliced

Juice of 1 lemon
(optional)

Cooked rice and fresh
coriander, to serve

1 Begin this meal the night before by soaking the lentils in enough cold water to cover them – approximately 300ml. When you're ready to cook, drain them and set aside.

2 Place a large pan over a low heat and add the oil. Stir in the onions, season with salt and freshly ground black pepper and cover with a layer of greaseproof paper and the pan lid. Sweat the onions for 10 minutes, stirring once or twice, until the onions are soft. Stir in the garlic and coriander, re-cover with the greaseproof paper and pan lid and sweat for a further 5 minutes.

3 Discard the greaseproof paper and stir in the lentils, chickpeas, tomatoes, cumin and harissa. Season and pour in the vegetable stock. Cover and bring to the boil. Reduce the heat and simmer, covered, for 25 minutes or until the lentils are tender and stew has thickened.

4 Stir in the olives and lemon juice, if using. Let the flavours mingle for a few minutes, then taste and adjust the seasoning if necessary. Serve the stew with rice cooked according to the packet instructions, and garnished with extra fresh coriander.

⏰ GET AHEAD >>
Cool the stew and divide between freezerproof containers. The stew will freeze for up to 3 months. To reheat, defrost completely and tip into a pan with an extra splash of vegetable stock. Warm over a medium heat until piping hot.

Turkey and broccoli stir-fry

A stir-fry makes a great quick meal and if you prepare and marinate the turkey the night before, you can have dinner ready in 10–15 minutes.

15 minutes to prepare + marinating | 10–15 minutes active cooking | Makes 2 servings

200g turkey breast, sliced into strips

½ tbsp cornflour

1 tsp Chinese 5 spice powder

5 tsp dark soy sauce

20g fresh ginger, peeled and grated

½ tbsp sunflower oil

150g broccoli, broken into small florets

8 spring onions, trimmed and chopped

50g cashew nuts

300ml hot chicken stock

3 tbsp rice wine or dry sherry

Cooked rice, to serve

1 Place the turkey in a non-metallic bowl with the cornflour, 5 spice powder, 2 tsp soy sauce and ginger. Stir to coat and marinate for 30 minutes at room temperature or overnight in the fridge.

2 Heat the oil in a wok or frying pan over a high heat. When the pan is very hot, add the turkey and stir-fry for 1–2 minutes or until starting to brown. Add the broccoli, spring onions and cashews and stir-fry for a further 2 minutes.

3 Carefully add the stock – the pan will steam – and the rice wine or dry sherry and the remaining soy sauce and simmer, stirring frequently, for 5–8 minutes or until the stock has reduced by ½ and the turkey is cooked through. Serve immediately with cooked rice.

Sesame beef stir-fry

A tasty stir-fry that's not only quick and easy, but makes great use of several lactogenic ingredients, too.

15 minutes to prepare + marinating | 8–10 minutes active cooking | Makes 2 servings

250g sirloin beef
steaks, sliced
into strips

1 clove garlic,
crushed

20g fresh ginger,
peeled and grated

1 tbsp soy sauce

1 tbsp rice wine
or dry sherry

1 tsp caster sugar

1 tsp cornflour

½ tbsp sunflower oil

200g fine green
beans, trimmed

150g carrot, peeled
and finely sliced

250ml hot vegetable
stock

150g cooked noodles

Handful of fresh
coriander leaves

Sesame seeds
and toasted sesame
oil, to serve

1 Place the beef in a non-metallic bowl with the garlic, ginger, soy sauce, rice wine or sherry, caster sugar and cornflour. Stir to coat and marinate for 30 minutes at room temperature or overnight in the fridge.

2 Heat the oil in a wok or frying pan over a high heat. When the pan is smoking hot, add the beef and stir-fry for 30 seconds. Add the green beans and carrot and stir-fry for a further 1 minute. Pour in the stock and any remaining marinade and bring to a simmer.

3 Reduce the heat and simmer for 5–8 minutes or until the sauce has thickened. Stir in the noodles and toss to mix. Stir-fry for a couple of minutes or until warmed through. Stir in a handful of fresh coriander leaves.

4 Divide between 2 serving plates, sprinkle over some sesame seeds and drizzle with toasted sesame oil to serve.

Venison steaks with beetroot relish

A special meal for two that doesn't involve hours of chopping and cooking – perfect!

15 minutes to prepare + marinating + resting | 4–8 minutes active cooking
| 15–20 minutes total cooking time | Makes 2 servings

2 x 200g venison steaks

1½ tbsp extra virgin olive oil

½ tbsp red wine vinegar

1 clove garlic, crushed

400g new potatoes

2 tsp softened butter

Watercress salad, to serve

Beetroot relish

150g cooked beetroot
(not stored in vinegar),
drained

1–2 tsp horseradish sauce

2 tsp red wine vinegar

A large handful of
fresh dill, finely chopped

1 Place the steaks in a non-metallic dish and drizzle over the oil and vinegar. Add the garlic and season with salt and freshly ground black pepper. Toss to coat, cover and chill for up to 3 hours.

2 While the steaks marinate, make the beetroot relish. Coarsely grate the beetroot and place in a bowl with 1–2 tsp horseradish sauce, adding more if you like it hotter, and the vinegar and dill. Season and stir to mix. Set aside.

3 Bring a pan of water to the boil. Add the potatoes and cook for 15–20 minutes or until they're tender.

4 Meanwhile, heat a heavy-based frying pan over a high heat. Once the pan is smoking hot, add the venison steaks and fry for 2–4 minutes each side, depending on how you like your steaks (cooking them beyond medium-rare may make them tough). Transfer the steaks to a plate, cover with foil and leave to rest somewhere warm.

5 Drain the potatoes, return to the pan and toss with the butter. Divide the potatoes between 2 warm serving plates with the beetroot relish and steaks. Drizzle over any venison juices and serve with a watercress salad.

⏰ GET AHEAD >>
The beetroot relish
can be made up to
24 hours ahead and
stored, covered,
in the fridge.

Sausage and fennel pies

Use good quality pork sausages in this chunky pie
for maximum flavour and satisfaction.

25 minutes to prepare | 10 minutes active cooking | 45 minutes total cooking time | Makes 4 servings

1½ tbsp extra virgin olive oil

6 pork sausages

1 onion, finely sliced

150g fennel bulb,
trimmed and sliced

1 x 400g can green lentils,
drained and rinsed

1 x 400g can
chopped tomatoes

1 tsp dried marjoram

300g potatoes,
scrubbed

Green vegetables,
to serve

1 Preheat the oven to gas mark 5/190°C/fan oven 170°C. Heat 1 tbsp of the oil in a frying pan over a medium heat. Add the sausages and fry, turning occasionally, until browned. Remove from the pan and set aside.

2 Add the onion to the pan, season with black pepper and fry for 5 minutes, stirring frequently, until starting to soften and brown. Add the fennel and continue to cook, stirring frequently, for 5 minutes or until the fennel has softened – add a splash of water to the pan if the fennel starts to stick.

3 Remove from the heat and stir in the lentils, tomatoes and marjoram. Chop the sausages and add to the mixture. Taste and adjust the seasoning, then spoon into 4 x 400ml ovenproof, freezerproof dishes. Set aside.

4 Slice the potatoes into thin rounds and lay over the top of the sausage and fennel mixture to cover. Brush with the remaining oil and then bake for 45 minutes or until golden, crisp and bubbling. Serve with steamed green vegetables.

⏰ GET AHEAD >>

The pies can be frozen once they've been assembled. Let them cool, then wrap in freezer film or cover with lids and freeze for up to 3 months. Cook from frozen at gas mark 5/190°C/fan oven 170°C for approximately 1 hour or until cooked through.

Salmon, dill and potato pies

An indulgent fish pie with a Scandinavian flavour, you can also swap the salmon for cod, haddock, pollack or a mixture.

45 minutes to prepare + cooling | 20 minutes active cooking | 1 hour total cooking time | Makes 4 servings

700g waxy potatoes, scrubbed

4 medium eggs

900g salmon fillets, skinned and chopped into small chunks

A large handful of fresh dill, chopped

300ml crème fraîche

25g butter, melted

Green vegetables or salad, to serve

1 Preheat the oven to gas mark 6/200°C/fan oven 180°C. Pour boiling water into a large pan and bring back to the boil. Add the whole potatoes and simmer for 15 minutes. Drain, cool under running cold water and set aside until cool enough to handle.

2 Meanwhile, cook the eggs in a separate pan of boiling water for 10 minutes, then transfer to a bowl of cold water and leave until cool enough to handle. Peel and quarter.

3 Divide the eggs and salmon between 4 x 400ml ovenproof, freezerproof containers. Season with freshly ground black pepper. Stir the dill into the crème fraîche and spoon over the salmon.

4 Coarsely grate the potatoes, including the skin. Stir the butter into the potatoes and season with salt and freshly ground black pepper. Spoon over the salmon and bake for 40–45 minutes or until golden, crisp and cooked through. Serve with steamed green vegetables or salad.

⏰ GET AHEAD >>

The pies can be frozen once they've been assembled. Let them cool, then wrap in freezer film or cover with lids and freeze for up to 3 months. Cook from frozen at gas mark 5/190°C/fan oven 170°C for approximately 45 minutes or until cooked through.

※

Sesame crusted fish fingers

Making your own fish fingers is easy and they're handy to have in your freezer for quick dinners.

25 minutes to prepare | 20 minutes active cooking | 40 minutes total cooking time | Makes 4 servings

4 large sweet potatoes, halved widthways and sliced into wedges

1 tbsp extra virgin olive oil

2 tsp paprika

40g white bread

4 tbsp sesame seeds

1 medium egg, beaten

2 tbsp plain flour

500g cod, haddock or pollack fillets

200g frozen peas, to serve

1 Preheat the oven to gas mark 6/200°C/fan oven 180°C.

2 Toss the sweet potato wedges with the oil, paprika and a pinch of salt. Arrange on a baking tray and roast for 40 minutes or until tender.

3 Meanwhile, blitz the bread in a food processor to make fine breadcrumbs. Tip onto a wide plate and mix in the sesame seeds. Pour the egg onto a shallow plate and sprinkle the flour onto another plate with some seasoning

4 Slice the fish into fingers about 10cm x 3cm – you should get about 12. Dip the fish fingers in the flour, then the egg and then the breadcrumbs to coat. Place on a baking tray greased with olive oil and bake for 20 minutes, turning once, or until cooked through.

5 Meanwhile, cook the peas in boiling water for 5 minutes or until tender.

6 Drain the peas and arrange on 4 warm serving plates with the fish fingers and potato wedges and serve.

⏰ **GET AHEAD >>**
The fish fingers can be frozen once they're assembled – open freeze on the baking tray until solid, then transfer to a freezerproof tub or freezer bag and freeze for up to 3 months. Cook from frozen at gas mark 6/200°C/fan oven 180°C for approximately 30–40 minutes.

Salmon and crab cakes

The combination of crab, salmon, chives and mustard make these fishcakes so tasty you won't be able to keep your hands off them!

35 minutes to prepare | 25 minutes total cooking time | Makes 6–8 servings

600g potatoes,
peeled and chopped

1 x 213g can red salmon
in brine

2 x 170g cans crab meat
in brine

2 spring onions, trimmed
and finely chopped

2 tbsp mayonnaise

A large handful of fresh
chives, finely chopped

½ tsp English
mustard powder

60g white bread

1 medium egg, beaten

2 tbsp plain flour

Sunflower oil,
for greasing

Watercress salad
and tartare sauce,
to serve

1 Preheat the oven to gas mark 6/200°C/fan oven 180°C. Bring a pan of water to the boil and add the potatoes. Simmer for 15 minutes or until tender. Drain and mash.

2 Drain the salmon and crab in a sieve and press with a fork to squeeze out as much liquid as possible. Add to the mashed potatoes with the spring onions, mayonnaise, chives and mustard powder. Using your hand, shape into 6–8 rounds and set aside.

3 Blitz the bread in a food processor to make fine breadcrumbs. Tip onto a wide plate. Pour the egg into a shallow bowl and sprinkle the flour onto a separate plate. Season the flour with a little salt and freshly ground black pepper.

4 Dip the fishcakes in the flour, and then the egg and then the breadcrumbs to coat on both sides, and place on a baking tray greased with sunflower oil. Bake for 20–25 minutes, turning once, or until golden brown and cooked through.

5 Serve the salmon and crab cakes with a watercress salad and tartare sauce.

⏰ **GET AHEAD >>**
The salmon and crab cakes can be frozen once they're assembled – open freeze on a baking tray until solid, then transfer to freezer bags or a freezerproof tub and freeze for up to 3 months. Cook from frozen at gas mark 6/200°C/fan oven 180°C for approximately 30–35 minutes.

Salt and pepper squid

One of my favourite take-away choices, this is surprisingly easy to make at home and gets a big thumbs-up from my husband. If you can't get whole squid, try making it with squid rings.

5–10 minutes to prepare | 8–10 minutes total cooking time | Makes 2 servings

1 tsp Chinese
5 spice powder

½ tsp chilli powder

½ tsp sea salt

1 tsp freshly ground
black pepper

1 tbsp plain flour

600g squid, cleaned
(ask your fishmonger
to do this)

2 tbsp sunflower oil

Sesame oil and sweet chilli
dipping sauce, to serve

1 Mix the 5 spice powder, chilli powder, salt, pepper and flour together. Set aside.

2 If your squid are large, cut their bodies open, wash and pat dry. Cut into squares. Rinse the tentacles and pat dry. Toss the squid in the spiced flour.

3 Heat the sunflower oil in a deep frying pan until very hot and add the squid. Fry for 1 minute on each side, in batches (don't crowd the pan) until the sides or tentacles begin to curl up.

4 Transfer to warm serving plates and drizzle with a little sesame oil. Serve with sweet chilli dipping sauce.

6
fast fishes

Cooking fish in foil parcels seals in the juices and saves on pots and pans – a huge bonus when you don't have much time.

All these recipes are easy to double, triple or more if you're cooking for more than yourself.

1 Sea bass with lemongrass and ginger

15 minutes to prepare | 30 minutes total cooking time | Makes 1 serving

Preheat the oven to gas mark 6/200°C/fan oven 180°C. Tear a 45cm long rectangle from a sheet of foil and brush with **sunflower oil**. Toss together **90g pak choi,** large leaves sliced, and **1 small carrot**, peeled and sliced into matchsticks, **a small handful of beansprouts**, **½ stick lemongrass**, halved, **10g fresh root ginger**, sliced into matchsticks, **1 red chilli**, deseeded and sliced, and **1 small garlic clove**, peeled and finely chopped. Season and arrange in the centre of the foil. Top with **1 x 100g fillet sea bass**. Season and drizzle over **a little sunflower oil**. Bring the long edges of the foil together and scrunch to seal. Scrunch the short ends together. Bake for 30 minutes or until the sea bass is cooked through. Discard the lemongrass and serve the fish with a drizzle of **sweet chilli dipping sauce**.

4 Cod and dill potatoes

8–10 minutes to prepare | 5 minutes active cooking | 25 minutes total cooking time | Makes 1 serving

Preheat the oven to gas mark 6/200°C/fan oven 180°C and put a pan of water on to boil. Tear a 45cm long rectangle from a sheet of foil and brush with **olive oil**. Slice **150g potatoes**, scrubbed, into rounds and plunge into the boiling water. Simmer for 5 minutes, then drain and arrange in the centre of the foil. Season and top with **2 spring onions**, sliced, and a **small handful of fresh dill sprigs**. Top with **1 x 200g cod loin**. Drizzle with **olive oil** and season. Bring the long edges of the foil together and scrunch to seal. Scrunch the short ends together. Bake for 20 minutes or until the cod is cooked all the way through and serve with a **green salad** or **green vegetables**.

2 Salmon and Swiss chard

10 minutes to prepare | 25 minutes total cooking time
| Makes 1 serving

Preheat the oven to gas mark 6/200°C/fan oven
180°C. Tear a 45cm long rectangle from a sheet of foil.
and brush with **olive oil**. Slice **50g Swiss chard** and
arrange in the centre of the foil. Season and top with
1 x 125g fillet salmon. Spread **1 tsp horseradish
sauce** over the salmon and drizzle over a little **lemon
juice** (optional). Season. Bring the long edges of the
foil together and scrunch to seal. Scrunch the short
ends together. Bake for 25 minutes or until the
salmon is cooked all the way through and serve
with **boiled new potatoes**.

3 Pollack and Jerusalem artichokes

10–15 minutes to prepare | 5 minutes active cooking
| 35 minutes total cooking time | Makes 1 serving

Preheat the oven to gas mark 6/200°C/fan oven
180°C. Peel and thinly slice **200g Jerusalem
artichokes** and cook in boiling water for 5 minutes.
Drain. Tear a 45cm long rectangle from a sheet of
foil and brush with **olive oil**. Arrange the Jerusalem
artichokes in the centre of the foil. Season and top
with **1 tsp capers**, drained, and **a few sprigs of fresh
tarragon**. Top with **1 x 175g skinless fillet pollack**
and drizzle with **olive oil**. Bring the long edges of
the foil together and scrunch to seal. Scrunch the
short ends together. Bake for 30 minutes or until
the pollack is cooked all the way through and
serve with a **watercress salad**.

5 Haddock and fennel

10 minutes to prepare | 30 minutes total cooking time
| Makes 1 serving

Preheat the oven to gas mark 6/200°C/fan oven
180°C. Tear a 45cm long rectangle from a sheet of
foil and brush with **olive oil**. Slice **80g fennel** and
arrange in the centre of the foil. Season and top
with **1 tbsp chopped fresh chives** and **150g
haddock fillet**. Drizzle over a little olive oil. Bring
the long edges of the foil together and scrunch
to seal. Scrunch the short ends together. Bake for
30 minutes or until the haddock is cooked all the
way through and serve with **boiled new potatoes**.

6 Hake with potatoes and peas

5–8 minutes to prepare | 5 minutes active cooking
| 25 minutes total cooking time | Makes 1 serving

Preheat the oven to gas mark 6/200°C/fan oven
180°C. Tear a 45cm long rectangle from a sheet
of foil and brush with **olive oil**. Slice **150g potatoes**,
scrubbed, into rounds and plunge into a pan of
boiling water. Cook for 5 minutes, then drain and
arrange in the centre of the foil with **50g peas**,
defrosted if frozen, and the grated zest of **½ lemon**.
Season and top with **1 x 150g fillet hake**. Drizzle
over **1 tbsp white wine vinegar** and bring the
long edges of the foil together and scrunch to seal.
Scrunch the short ends together. Bake for 25 minutes
or until the hake is cooked all the way through and
serve with **tartare sauce**.

Sweet things

I'm a big believer that a little of what you fancy does you good, especially when it comes to the Apricot and cardamom crumble on page 74.

V ✲

Apricot and cardamom crumble

A traditional pud with a spicy twist, this crumble will sit happily in the fridge for a couple of days after cooking or it can be frozen ready to bake.

20 minutes to prepare | 25–30 minutes total cooking time | Makes 4–6 servings

4 cardamom pods

150g caster sugar

2 tsp cornflour

550g apricots, halved, stoned and chopped

Crumble topping

150g plain flour

150g caster sugar

150g cold unsalted butter, chopped

100g porridge oats

50g flaked almonds

Yogurt, cream, custard or ice cream, to serve

1 Preheat the oven to gas mark 6/200°C/fan oven 180°C. Pound the cardamom pods with a pestle to separate the seeds from the green, papery skins. Discard the skins and grind the seeds to a fine powder. Mix with the sugar and cornflour in a large bowl, then stir in the apricots. Spoon into a 1½ litre ovenproof dish.

2 Make the crumble topping. Sift the flour into a large mixing bowl and stir in the sugar. Rub in the butter with your fingertips to make fine crumbs. Stir in the oats and flaked almonds.

3 Sprinkle the crumble over the apricots, making sure they're well covered. Bake for 25–30 minutes or until golden and bubbling. Serve warm or cold on its own or with yogurt, cream, custard or ice cream.

⏰ **GET AHEAD >>**
You can freeze the crumble once it's assembled in its dish and bake it from frozen. It'll take about 50 minutes to cook. Alternatively, cook and cool the crumble and then divide between freezerproof containers and freeze. Defrost and reheat in the microwave.

V 🥕 ⊛

Almond rice pudding

This vegan rice pudding has all the creamy flavours you expect from the traditional version but it's made with almond milk. Try it with a spoonful of strawberry jam.

5–10 minutes to prepare | 1½–2 hours total cooking time | Makes 4 servings

Almond butter,
for greasing

110g short grain
pudding rice

700ml almond milk

50g caster sugar

1 tsp ground cinnamon

Freshly grated nutmeg

Jam, to serve

1 Preheat the oven to gas mark 2/150°C/fan oven 130°C. Spread 1–2 tsp almond butter over the base of a 1½ litre ovenproof dish and set aside.

2 Rinse the rice under cold running water and shake off any excess water. Tip into the dish and pour over the almond milk. Stir in the caster sugar. Sprinkle the top with the ground cinnamon and a pinch of freshly grated nutmeg. Don't worry if it looks really liquidy – the rice will absorb most of it.

3 Bake the pudding for 30 minutes, then stir and bake for a further 1–1½ hours, checking every 10 minutes after the first hour, until it's just set and still a little wobbly in the middle if you give the dish a gentle shake.

4 Let the rice pudding rest for 10–15 minutes at room temperature before serving with a spoonful of jam.

Turn to page 24 for an easy recipe for almond butter and page 92 for almond milk.

⏰ **GET AHEAD >>**
The rice pudding will keep in the fridge for 3–4 days and is very moreish eaten cold.

Quick oat and ginger crunch

I ate a simpler version of this dessert almost daily when I was breastfeeding my daughter – I was always starving and it made a great snack! I've added stem ginger for a bit more spice and seeds to give it extra crunch.

2 minutes to prepare | Makes 1 serving

150g Greek yogurt

2 Nairn's Stem
Ginger Oat Biscuits

1 piece stem ginger
in syrup, drained

1–2 tsp pumpkin or
sunflower seeds

1 Spoon the yogurt into a small bowl and bash the biscuits with a pestle or the end of a rolling pin to make small chunks and crumbs. Sprinkle over the yogurt.

2 Finely chop the stem ginger and sprinkle over the biscuits with a few pumpkin or sunflower seeds. Eat straight away.

v

Peach and raspberry trifle

For some women chocolate can be anti-lactogenic, but this trifle stretches out the flavour of the cocoa powder without overdosing on chocolate. It's a very good-natured trifle and will sit happily in the fridge for a few days.

25 minutes to prepare + chilling | Makes 6 servings

250g mascarpone cheese

300g Greek yogurt

1 tsp vanilla extract

2 tbsp icing sugar

225g trifle sponges or sponge fingers

1 x 410g can peaches in syrup, drained and syrup reserved

170g raspberries

1 tbsp cocoa powder

1 Beat the mascarpone with the yogurt, vanilla and icing sugar. Set aside.

2 Dip half the trifle sponges in the reserved peach syrup to soak them and use them to line a 1 litre serving dish. Place half the peaches and raspberries on top of the sponges and then spoon over half the mascarpone mix. Sift over ½ tbsp of the cocoa powder.

3 Dip the remaining sponge fingers in the peach syrup and arrange on top of the mascarpone. Cover with the remaining peach slices and raspberries. Spoon over the mascarpone mixture and sift the remaining cocoa powder over the top.

4 Chill for 24 hours before serving.

⏰ **GET AHEAD >>**
You can eat this trifle after a few hours chilling, but it's best after a day in the fridge. It'll keep well for 2–3 days

V ❄

Coconut fairy cakes

Keep a batch of these cute cakes in your freezer and wow your friends when they come round to admire the new baby.

25 minutes to prepare | 20–25 minutes total cooking time | Makes 18 fairy cakes

75g butter, softened
160ml coconut cream
125g caster sugar
2 eggs, beaten
1 tsp vanilla extract
150g self-raising flour
50g desiccated coconut

Cream cheese frosting
75g butter, softened
150g full fat cream cheese
60g icing sugar, sifted
Silver balls, to decorate

1 Preheat the oven to gas mark 4/180°C/fan oven 160°C.
Line 2 x 12-hole bun tins with 18 paper cake cases and set aside.

2 Beat the butter, coconut cream and sugar together until soft and creamy. Beat in the eggs, a little at a time, then stir in the vanilla extract. Sift in the flour and add the desiccated coconut. Fold in to combine.

3 Spoon the cake batter into the cake cases and bake for 20–25 minutes or until the cakes are risen, golden and springy to the touch – a skewer inserted in the middle should come out clean. Cool on a wire rack.

4 Make the cream cheese frosting. Beat the butter until it's soft and creamy and then beat in the cream cheese. Sift in the icing sugar and stir to make a thick icing.

5 Spread the icing over the fairy cakes with a palette knife so they're thickly covered and decorate with little silver balls. The cakes will keep, un-iced, in an airtight tin for 2–3 days and the icing will keep in the fridge for the same amount of time.

⏰ GET AHEAD >>
To freeze these cakes, pop around 4 into a freezer bag and freeze for up to 3 months. Defrost overnight and either eat them un-iced, drizzled with glacé icing or topped with the cream cheese frosting.

V ❄

Beetroot, pecan and sultana cake

A deliciously moist cake that's subtly sweet and stores really well.
It's good plain or try it buttered for breakfast.

25 minutes to prepare | 50 minutes–1 hour total cooking time | Makes 8–10 slices

150g coconut oil,
plus extra for greasing

175g caster sugar

2 medium eggs, beaten

2 tbsp whole milk

150g self-raising flour

1 tsp ground ginger

1 tsp ground cinnamon

250g cooked beetroot
(not stored in vinegar),
coarsely grated

100g pecans,
roughly chopped

75g sultanas

1 Preheat the oven to gas mark 5/190°C/fan oven 170°C. Grease a loaf tin with a little coconut oil and line the base with baking parchment. Set aside.

2 Melt the coconut oil over a low heat if it's solid and then pour into a large mixing bowl. Whisk in the sugar until the mixture is light and frothy, then whisk in the eggs and the milk.

3 Sift the flour, ginger and cinnamon into the mixing bowl and stir until combined. Fold in the beetroot, pecans and sultanas and spoon the cake mixture into the prepared tin. Bake for 50 minutes–1 hour or until risen and firm to the touch – a skewer inserted in the middle should come out clean.

4 Cool in the tin for 15 minutes, then turn out onto a wire rack to cool completely. Serve in slices.

⏰ **GET AHEAD >>**
Wrap the cake in foil and store in an airtight container. It will keep for 3–5 days wrapped. It can also be frozen for up to 3 months.

Apricot and ginger flapjacks

These scrumptious flapjacks will give you an energy boost
that'll keep you going between meals.

20 minutes to prepare | 30–40 minutes active cooking | 50 minutes–1 hour total cooking time | Makes 10 flapjacks

250g soft, dried
ready-to-eat apricots

450ml cold water

Sunflower oil, for greasing

100g porridge oats

100g barley flakes

50g crystallised ginger,
finely chopped

3 tbsp pumpkin seeds

3 tbsp sunflower seeds

2 tbsp sesame seeds

1 tbsp milled flaxseed

1 tsp ground ginger

2 tbsp golden syrup

1 Place the apricots in a pan with the cold water, cover and bring to a simmer. Remove the lid and simmer gently for 20–30 minutes or until the apricots are plump and juicy and most of the water has been absorbed. Set aside to cool.

2 Preheat the oven to gas mark 4/180°C/fan oven 160°C. Lightly grease the base of a 20cm square cake tin with sunflower oil and line with baking parchment. Set aside. Place the oats, barley flakes, crystallised ginger, all the seeds and the ground ginger in a large bowl.

3 Purée the apricots in a food processor or with a hand-held blender until smooth. Stir the purée into the oat mixture with the golden syrup. Spoon into the cake tin, pressing down to evenly cover the tin.

4 Bake for 30 minutes or until firm and golden brown. Mark into 10 flapjack bars and leave to cool completely in the tin. When the flapjacks are cold, turn out of the tin, peel off the paper and separate into bars to serve.

⏰ GET AHEAD >>

The flapjacks will keep for a week in an airtight tin.

V ❄

Almond drop cookies

These American-style cookies make a great sweet snack
and they look pretty stylish, too. If you don't have flaked almonds,
just press the cookies with a fork to flatten slightly before cooking.

20–25 minutes to prepare + chilling | 20 minutes total cooking time | Makes 32–40 cookies

200g plain flour

½ tsp baking powder

150g ground almonds

250g butter, softened

100g caster sugar

2 medium eggs, beaten

**Flaked almonds,
to decorate**

1 Sift the flour and baking powder into a bowl and stir in the ground almonds and a small pinch of salt. Set aside.

2 Beat the butter and sugar together until creamy. Beat in the eggs, a little at a time, until combined.

3 Gradually stir in the flour to make a soft dough. Spoon into a bowl, cover and chill for 45 minutes or until the dough has just firmed up.

4 Preheat the oven to gas mark 5/190°C/fan oven 170°C. Drop 32–40 teaspoonfuls of cookie dough onto 2–4 baking trays, making sure they are well spaced apart. Lightly press a flaked almond into the middle of each cookie. Bake for 20 minutes or until a light golden brown – they will spread slightly as they cook.

5 Lift the cookies from the baking trays with a palette knife and transfer to a wire rack to cool and crisp up before serving. Store the cookies in an airtight tin – they will keep for up to 3 days.

⏰ **GET AHEAD >>**
The uncooked cookie dough can be frozen for up to 3 months, ready to bake. Drop teaspoonfuls of the cookie dough onto baking trays, press down lightly with a fork and open freeze until solid. Leave the cookies on the tray for 1 minute at room temperature, then lift off with a palette knife and store in freezer bags. Bake the cookies from frozen as above for 20–25 minutes.

V ❄

Fig and walnut cookies

The combination of figs, walnuts and fennel seeds
in these cookies is irresistibly good. Gorgeous on their own
or try them with vanilla ice cream for added indulgence.

40 minutes to prepare + freezing | 12–15 minues total cooking time | Makes 56 cookies

300g plain flour

1½ tsp baking powder

300g butter, softened

250g soft light
brown sugar

3 medium eggs, beaten

200g soft, dried
ready-to-eat figs,
finely chopped

200g walnuts, chopped

1 tsp fennel seeds

1 Sift the flour and baking powder into a bowl and stir in a small pinch
of salt. Set aside.

2 Beat the butter and sugar together until creamy, then beat in the eggs,
a little at a time, until combined.

3 Stir in the figs, walnuts and fennel seeds. Fold in the flour to make
a thick, sticky dough.

4 Divide the dough into 4 and shape into 4 logs, approximately 15cm long
and 4cm high. Wrap in a double layer of freezerwrap and freeze for 1 hour
or until firm. Preheat the oven to gas mark 5/190°C/fan oven 170°C.

5 Using a sharp knife, slice the logs of chilled cookie dough into 1cm thick
rounds and place the cookies on 4 large baking trays, well spaced apart.
Bake for 12–15 minutes or until golden – the cookies will spread a lot
as they bake.

6 Lift the cookies off the baking tray with a palette knife and transfer
to a wire rack to cool. Eat within 3 days.

⏰ **GET AHEAD >>**

The dough freezes really well. Slice the logs into 1cm thick cookies and open
freeze on baking trays or plates until solid. Store the cookies in freezer bags
for up to 3 months. Bake them from frozen. They'll take approximately
15 minutes at gas mark 5/190°C/fan oven 170°C.

Drinks

Including lactogenic foods in your day is even easier
with these refreshing drinks, especially the fruit
and vegetable smoothies on pages 90–91.

⊛ **V**

chai spiced milk

This Indian-inspired hot drink makes a soothing alternative to tea.

3 minutes to prepare | 3–4 minutes active cooking | Makes 1 serving

300ml whole milk

1 cinnamon stick

3 cardamom pods

1 slice of fresh ginger

3 cloves

½ tsp fennel seeds

½ tsp black peppercorns

1 Place the milk and spices in a small pan over a low heat. Gently warm, stirring constantly, until the milk is steaming hot but not boiling.

2 Pour the milk through a sieve into a heatproof glass or mug and serve.

12
speedy smoothies

when you're short on time but in need of a boost, blitz up a smoothie. For a lot of these smoothies you can just chuck the ingredients into the blender with barely any prep, making them perfect for quick breakfasts or stop-gap snacks on busy days.

V 🥕

1 Fig, almond and oat

5 minutes to prepare | Serves 1

Blitz **3 fresh figs**, woody stalks removed, **2 tbsp porridge oats, 1 tsp maple syrup, 200ml almond milk** and **2 tbsp almond milk pulp** until smooth.

V ⊛

4 Mango and peach

10 minutes to prepare | Serves 1

Blitz **1 peach**, halved and stoned, **½ medium mango**, peeled, stoned and chopped, **200ml whole milk, 2 tbsp natural yogurt** and **1 tsp milled flaxseed** until smooth.

V ⊛

7 Dried fruit and pumpkin seed

5 minutes to prepare | Serves 1

Blitz **2 soft, dried ready-to-eat figs, 2 soft, dried ready-to-eat apricots, 2 dried, pitted, ready-to-eat dates, 1 tsp pumpkin seeds, 250ml whole milk** and **1 tbsp natural yogurt** until smooth.

V ⊛

10 Mango and ginger

5–8 minutes to prepare | Serves 1

Blitz **½ medium mango**, peeled, stoned and chopped, **2 pieces crystallised stem ginger, 200ml whole milk** and **1 tbsp natural yogurt** until smooth.

V

2 Fig, peach and sesame

5 minutes to prepare | Serves 1

Blitz **1 peach**, halved and stoned, with **2 fresh figs**, woody stalks removed, **1 tsp sesame seeds**, **1 tsp tahini**, **200ml whole milk**, **2 tbsp natural yogurt** and **1 tsp clear honey** until smooth.

V

5 Apricot, strawberry and flaxseed

5–8 minutes to prepare | Serves 1

Blitz **2 apricots**, peeled and stoned, **100g strawberries**, **1 tsp milled flaxseed**, **200ml whole milk** and **2 tbsp natural yogurt** until smooth.

V

8 Apricot, oat and almond

5 minutes to prepare | Serves 1

Blitz **2 apricots**, halved and stoned, **15g whole almonds**, **200ml oat milk**, **1 tsp maple syrup** and **a pinch of ground ginger** until smooth.

V

11 Pear, fennel and carrot

8–10 minutes to prepare | Serves 1

Blitz **1 pear**, peeled, cored and chopped, with **75g fresh fennel**, chopped, and **250ml carrot juice** until smooth. Pour through a sieve to serve.

🧑‍🍳 KITCHEN TIP

You can skip the sieving stage, but the drink will separate after 5 minutes and you'll need to stir it back together to drink. Alternatively, make it in a juicer for a smoother drink.

V

3 Plum, oat and cinnamon

5 minutes to prepare | Serves 1

Blitz **3 plums**, halved and stoned, **200ml oat milk**, **2 tbsp oat milk pulp** and **a pinch of ground cinnamon** until smooth.

V

6 Peach, plum and almond

5 minutes to prepare | Serves 1

Blitz **1 peach**, halved and stoned, **1 plum**, halved and stoned, **200ml almond milk** and **2 tbsp almond milk pulp** with **1 tsp milled flaxseed** until smooth.

V

9 Peach, raspberry and oat

5 minutes to prepare | Serves 1

Blitz **1 peach**, halved and stoned, **75g raspberries**, **1 tsp maple syrup** and **200ml oat milk** until smooth.

V

12 Beetroot, pear and carrot

5–8 minutes to prepare | Serves 1

Blitz **50g cooked beetroot** (not stored in vinegar), chopped, with **1 medium pear**, peeled, cored and chopped, and **250ml carrot juice** until smooth.

🧑‍🍳 KITCHEN TIP

This smoothie will separate after 5–10 minutes and you'll need to stir it back together to drink.

V 🥕 ⊛ ❄

3 dairy-free milks

Nut milks make a nutritious alternative to the usual dairy milks and they're widely available in health food shops and supermarkets, but they're also easy to make yourself and they freeze really well, too.

1 Almond milk

10 minutes to prepare + overnight soaking
| Makes 1½ litres

Place **250g whole almonds** in a large bowl with **1½ litres cold water**. Cover and soak overnight. To make the milk, place the water and almonds in a large blender and add **4 dried, pitted, ready-to-eat dates**. Blitz until the almonds are finely chopped and the milk is fairly smooth – you may need to do this in batches. Pour the milk through a sieve in batches, pressing the pulp to squeeze out as much milk as possible. Store the milk in a sterilised jar or bottle in the fridge.

🍞 KITCHEN TIP

The leftover almond pulp will keep for a few days or can also be frozen. Add it to smoothies and porridge or make a quick dessert by stirring in some chopped dark or milk chocolate, drizzling with honey and serving with a spoonful of yogurt.

2 Oat milk

15 minutes to prepare + overnight soaking
| Makes 900ml

Place **200g rolled porridge oats** in a blender or food processor with **1 litre cold water** and blitz to combine. Pour into a jug and leave overnight. In the morning, pour the mixture through a sieve in batches, using a spoon to press the oats to squeeze out as much milk as possible. Store the milk in a sterilised jar or bottle in the fridge. Sweeten with **maple syrup** to serve.

🍞 KITCHEN TIP

The oat milk will keep for 3–5 days in the fridge or it can be frozen for up to 3 months. The leftover oats can be used in smoothies, stirred into porridges, casseroles, stews or breads. Please note oat milk is low in gluten but it isn't gluten-free.

3 Cashew nut milk

15 minutes to prepare + overnight soaking | Makes 1½ litres

Place **300g cashew nuts** in a bowl and cover with **1½ litres cold water**. Leave to soak overnight. Pour the water and cashews into a blender and blitz until smooth – you may need to do this in batches. Pour the mixture through a sieve in batches, pressing the cashews to squeeze out as much milk as possible. Store the milk in a sterilised jar or bottle in the fridge. Sweeten with **maple syrup** to serve.

🍞 KITCHEN TIP

Use the leftover cashew nut pulp in porridges, smoothies and curries.

⏰ GET AHEAD >>

All the milks will keep for 3–5 days in the fridge or can be frozen for up to 3 months. Freeze small amounts in ice cube trays for adding to smoothies or pour into freezerproof containers or small milk cartons to freeze a pint at a time.

V 🥕 ⊛

5 herbal teas

Caffeine can have an anti-lactogenic effect, which may mean forgoing tea or coffee. These herbal teas can all be as refreshing as your usual cuppa.

1 Fenugreek seed tea

5 minutes to steep | Makes 1 serving

Place **2 tsp fenugreek seeds** in a heatproof jug and cover with **300ml boiling water**. Cover and set aside for 5 minutes, then strain into a mug or cup.

2 Fennel and caraway seed tea

5 minutes to steep | Makes 1 serving

Place **½ tsp fennel seeds** and **½ tsp caraway seeds** in a heatproof jug and cover with **300ml boiling water**. Cover and set aside for 5 minutes, then strain into a mug or cup.

3 Umbel seed tea

5 minutes to steep | Makes 1 serving

Place **¼ tsp fennel seeds**, **½ tsp caraway seeds**, **½ tsp aniseed** and **½ tsp dill seed** in a heatproof jug and cover with **300ml boiling water**. Cover and set aside for 5 minutes, then strain into a mug or cup.

4 Fresh ginger tea

2 minutes to prepare | 5 minutes to steep | Makes 2 servings

Coarsely grate **25g fresh root ginger** (no need to peel) and place in a teapot. Fill the teapot with **600ml boiling water** and set aside for 5 minutes to steep. The longer the tea steeps, the more fiery it becomes. You can reuse the same ginger 2–3 times, the tea will just get milder with each pot.

5 Fresh nettle tea

2 minutes to prepare + picking | 5–10 minutes to steep | Makes 1 serving

Wearing gloves, snip **a handful of the small top leaves from nettle plants** located away from traffic, pesticides and animal waste (the bigger, darker, older leaves will have a bitter taste compared to the top leaves). Rinse the leaves in cold water to get rid of any insects. Snip with scissors and place in a heatproof jug or teapot. Cover with **300ml boiling water** and set aside to steep for 5–10 minutes. Strain into a cup and drink by itself or with a **slice of lemon** and **maple syrup**.

Stockists

All the recipes in *The Contented Calf Cookbook* have been designed to be easy to make and easy to shop for, but we've come up with a list of stockists you might find helpful when you're shopping for lactogenic ingredients.

Biona
www.biona.co.uk
An organic food company whose range includes organic, raw, cooking-grade coconut oil.

G Baldwin & Co
171–173 Walworth Road,
London SE17 1RW
020 7703 5550
www.baldwins.co.uk
Independent London herbalist and wholefood store with an easy-to-use website for online shopping.

Beanfreaks
www.beanfreaks.com
A mini chain of health food stores with shops in Cardiff, Newport, Cwmbran and Bridgend.

Coconoil
www.coconoil.co.uk
Organic and virgin cooking-grade coconut oil.

Goodness Direct
www.goodnessdirect.co.uk
Online grocer that's particularly good for people with restricted diets.

Greenlife
1–2 Birdwood Court, High Street,
Totnes, Devon TQ9 5SG
01803 866 738, www.greenlife.co.uk
Natural products store based in Totnes and with an online shop.

The Hive Honey Shop
93 Northcote Road, London SW11 6PL
020 7924 6233, www.thehivehoneyshop.co.uk
Honey specialists with an exhaustive range of British, gourmet and international honeys.

Holland & Barrett
www.hollandandbarrett.com
International chain of wholefood shops. Particularly good for dried fruits, nuts, seeds, grains and honey.

Julian Graves
www.juliangraves.com
National chain of wholefood shops with a huge range of dried fruits, cereals, pulses, grains, nuts, seeds and honey.

National Association of Health Stores
www.nahs.co.uk
The National Association of Health Food Stores, established in 1931. The website includes a store locator so you can find your nearest independent store.

The Nutri Centre
020 8752 8450, www.nutricentre.com
A national chain of alternative health and wholefood stores. Foods include cooking-grade coconut oils.

Out Of This World
www.ootw.co.uk
A mini chain with shops in Leeds, Nottingham and Newcastle as well as an online store selling ethically sourced foods.

Real Foods
37 Broughton Street, Edinburgh EH1 3JU
and 8 Broughton Street, Toll Cross EH3 9JH
www.realfoods.co.uk
Scotland's largest organic retailer with two branches in Edinburgh and an online shop. Nuts, seeds, spices and dried herbs as well as fresh and frozen foods.

The Spice Shop
1 Blenheim Crescent, London W11 2EE
020 7221 4448, www.thespiceshop.co.uk
Specialist spice store selling every spice and dried herb you can imagine.

Further reading

Books

The Breastfeeding Mother's Guide to Making More Milk Diana West and Lisa Marasco (McGraw-Hill, £12.99),
www.lowmilksupply.org

The Food of Love: your formula for successful breastfeeding
Kate Evens (Myriad Editions, £12.99)
www.thefoodoflove.org

Mother Food: A Breastfeeding Diet Guide with Lactogenic Foods and Herbs for a Mom and Baby's Best Health
Hilary Jacobson (Rosalind Press, £10.99)
www.mother-food.com

The New Breastfeeding Diet Plan: Breakthrough ways to reduce toxins and give your baby the best start in life
Robert Rountree and Melissa Block
(McGraw-Hill, £9.99)

Websites

www.holistic-herbalist.com
/galactagogue-and-lactation-herbs.html
Galactagogue and Lactation Herbs For Increasing Breast Milk Production

www.mobimotherhood.org
MOBI Motherhood International
(Mothers Overcoming Breastfeeding Issues)

www.drjaygordon.com
/breastfeeding/increasing-milk-supply.html
Mother's Milk, How to Increase Your Supply

References

DHA and breast milk: goodies for baby's brain. Retrieved 13 October 2010, from 007 Breasts: http://www.007b.com/breastfeeding_intelligence_diet.php

Ben-Jonathan, N., & Hnasko, R. (2001, December). *Dopamine as a prolactin (PRL) inhibitor*. Retrieved 13 October 2010, from PubMed.gov: U.S. National Library of Medicine: http://www.ncbi.nlm.nih.gov/pubmed/11739329

Bonyata, K. (30 March 2010). *How does milk production work?* Retrieved 11 October 2010, from kellymom: breastfeeding & parenting: www.kellymom.com/bf/supply/milkproduction.html

Broadhurst, C. L., & Duke PhD, J. A. *Saponin: Natural Steroids*. Retrieved 13 October 2010, from The Herb Companion: www.herbcompanion.com/print-article.aspx?id=6710

Chen, P. J. (22 October 2008). *Your baby's first few weeks – Breast Milk – The Basics*. Retrieved October 2010, from University of Maryland Medical Center: www.umm.edu/pregnancy/000115.html

Definition of Dopamine. (19 March 2004). *Definition of Dopamine*. Retrieved 13 October 2010, from MedicineNet.com - We Bring Doctor's Knowledge to You: www.medterms.com/script/main/art.asp?articlekey=14345

Evens, K. (2009). *The Food of Love: your formula for successful breastfeeding.* Brighton: Myriad Editions: 10

Hareyan, A. (26 September 2004). *Coconut Oil Increases Beneficial Properties in Human Breast Milk*. Retrieved 13 October 2010, from EmaxHealth: http://www.emaxhealth.com/4/689.html

Jacobson, H. (2007). *Mother Food: A Breastfeeding Diet Guide with Lactogenic Foods and Herbs for a Mom and Baby's Best Health*. Rosalind Press: 6, 24- 44, 96, 118-123, 126-136, 144-153, 160-163

Kimball, J. W. (14 November 2009). *Hormones of the Pituitary*. Retrieved 13 October 2010, from Kimball's Biology Pages: http://users.rcn.com/jkimball.ma.ultranet/BiologyPages/P/Pituitary.html

Makina, D. M., & Krasnovskaia, I. A. (1999). *Morphofunctional characteristics of rat thyroid gland under the combined effect of oxytocin and adrenaline*. Retrieved 13 October 2010, from PubMed.gov: U.S. National Library of Medicine: http://www.ncbi.nlm.nih.gov/pubmed/10561851

Letdown Reflex When Breastfeeding. Retrieved 13 October 2010, from Kid & Parent: Every Parent Should Know: http://www.kidandparent.in/babycare/feeding/letdown-reflex-when-breastfeeding

Prentice, A. (1996, December). *Food and Nutrition bulletin – Volume 17*, Number 4, December 1996. Retrieved 1 November 2010, from The United Nations University Press: Food and Nutrition Bulletin: http://archive.unu.edu/unupress/food/8F174e/8F174E04.htm#Constituentsofhumanmilk

Rountree, R., & Block, M. (2006). *The New Breastfeeding Diet Plan: Breakthrough ways to reduce toxins and give your baby the best start in life*. McGraw-Hill.

WebMD Medical Reference. (25 February 2010). *Why Breakfast Is the Most Important Meal of the Day*. Retrieved 1 November 2010, from WebMD Medical Reference: http://www.webmd.com/diet/guide/most-important-meal

West, D., & Marasco, L. (2009). *The Breastfeeding Mother's Guide to Making More Milk*. McGraw-Hill.

Weston, S. (28 September 2010). *A third of people in Ireland skip breakfast*. Retrieved 26 October 2010, from FoodBev.com: http://www.foodbev.com/report/a-third-of-people-in-ireland-skip-breakfast

Whittlestone, W. G. (1954). *The effect of adrenaline on the milk-ejection response of the sow – Whittlestone 10 (2): 167*. Retrieved 13 October 2010, from Journal of Endocrinology: http://joe.endocrinology-journals.org/cgi/content/abstract/10/2/167

Index

Index

Thank yous

This cookbook was dreamt up during the many hours I spent feeding my daughter. Thanks to a lot of special people it made the leap from dream into reality.

First up, thank you to the totally fabulous Jassy Davis, without whom this book wouldn't be half of what it is now. Her expertise, enthusiasm and dedication have been invaluable and overwhelming. Here's to our joint success!

I'd also like to thank Helen Armstrong, Tony Briscoe, Jon Harvey, Sophie Joyce, Hannah Minney, Sara Ross, Penny Stephens, Clara Stevenson and Rick Stevenson, all of whom have been key members of the extended Contented Calf family. Thank you for bringing *The Contented Calf Cookbook* to life.

Thank you to everyone who's undertaken research into the link between successful breastfeeding and diet. Your work inspired me and enabled me to create this book. This is especially true of Hilary Jacobson, Diana West and Lisa Marasco.

Thank you to my NCT 'ladies and babies'. I'm sure my successful breastfeeding experience is down to having such a great group of girls to go through it with. To go from meeting someone for the first time to, weeks later, being able to completely expose your breast while you position your babe's head ready for latching on is pretty intense. Thanks for making that experience so secure, comfortable and filled with laughter. In particular, thank you to Diana for being my daily "I'm so glad you said that!" partner on our walks to nursery.

And thanks to my wider circle of friends who have encouraged and supported me not only in creating this book, but in life generally. Special thanks to Kate, Sue and Nikki – I couldn't do it without you, thanks for keeping me sane.

Thanks to my wonderful family. Your love, laughter, security and encouragement have been instrumental in giving me the courage to start such a crazy project. Thank you for everything, especially 'MummyAnne', whose phrase: "Contented cow, contented calf" gave birth to Contented Calf the company.

And finally, to the two people without whom none of this would've started. Al, you're my number one fan and support me 100% in everything I do, believing in me even when I don't believe in myself. Thank you for supporting me in getting Contented Calf off the ground. I honestly couldn't have done it without you. I love you and I'm honoured to share my life with you.

And Evelyn, your entrance into this world turned Mummy and Daddy's life completely upside down. Your zest for life from day one has been an inspiration to me. I love you more than I can ever say and my heart just bursts with pride every time I look at you. I hope that by starting Contented Calf I can make you proud, too.

Thank you everyone.

Lightning Source UK Ltd.
Milton Keynes UK
UKIC01n0301310314
229048UK00010B/57